EVERYDAY BOOK OF INSIGHTS

World Wisdom and Philosophy
for Purpose Balance
Inspiration and Happiness

Annette Kingsley

MINDFUL WISDOM MEDIA AND PUBLISHING

Copyright © 2012 by Annette Kingsley

All rights reserved. No part of this publication may be reproduced, distributed, or transmitted in any form or by any means, including photocopying, recording, or other electronic or mechanical methods, without the prior written permission of the publisher, except in the case of brief quotations embodied in critical reviews and certain other noncommercial uses permitted by copyright law. For permission requests, write to the publisher at the address below.

The author of this book does not dispense medical advice or prescribe the use of any technique as a form of treatment for physical or medical problems without the advice of a physician, either directly or indirectly. The intent of the author is only to offer information of a general nature to help you in your quest for emotional and spiritual wellbeing. In the event you use any of the information in this book for yourself, the author and the publisher assume no responsibility for your actions.

Mindful Wisdom Media & Publishing
Office 8, 10 Buckhurst Road
Bexhill-on-Sea
East Sussex
TN40 1QF
Tel: 01424 73 53 93

www.mindful-wisdom-media-and-publishing.com
E-mail: books@mindful-wisdom-media-and-publishing.com

First Edition
  ISBN: 978-0-9572673-0-5

Cover design by Amplitude Creative
www.amplitudecreative.co.uk

Cover photo chosen by Annette Kingsley
Interior Typography by Annette Kingsley
Typefaces: Philosopher & Gandhi Serif

Dedicated

to my daughters

Kioko-Amari and Miyuki,

the beautiful jewels in my everyday.

To Abby

Wishing you much love, magic & happiness on your new horizons. And may you be blessed with abundance, health & peace.

Acknowledgements...

Oaklyn, thank-you for your patience, assistance and understanding and your spirited belief in my ongoing purpose and motivation for the work for which I am inescapably drawn, also to my parents for you are all the foundation of it all.

Special thank-you's to: TR Johnson and Darren Pugh for some sterling assistance with the never ending proofing. Sophie Purser for those finishing touches when I needed some help, Chris Gill for your kind support and expertise and Mark Leatherland for creativity, patience and vision.

A heartfelt thank-you to everyone that has supported, encouraged, advised and contributed to the completion of this book. You have made the journey possible.

Thank-you to everyone that has read the blog, commented, e-mailed or in some way fuelled the ongoing work on mindful wisdom. It is one thing when it is just you but it is quite another when you are part of an extraordinary group of individuals all indelibly linked to the path of a greater self. You are the reason for the book and you are what makes all the hard work worthwhile. Together we follow the way where ever it may lead us, through the superb to the sublime but always a truly exceptional voyage.

Finally, thank-you to my daughters for providing me with those quintessential life lessons, moments of deep challenge and side splitting humour. And above all offering the place for unconditional love, where would I be without you?

What people are saying about the Everyday Book of Insights...

"I found Every Day Book of Insights very inspiring, in places so simple but at the same time deeply profound. I really loved it." - *Geoff Thompson, Bafta winning writer, teacher, martial artist www.geoffthompson.com*

Everyday Book of Insights, is the perfect little pick me up on a grey day. All of us can use a moment of wisdom and perspective in life which this lovely book delivers. Whether you use it to stay grounded or to spark deep, fulfilling conversations, you can trust that it will deliver what you need. I recommend you regularly just pick it up and turn to the first page you come to! Annette Kingsley's nuggets of wisdom promise to keep you focused on moving gracefully through your life." - *Zen DeBrucke Author, The Smart Soul: Transforming Stress and Anxiety into Success and Fulfillment www.thesmartsoul.com*

"I absolutely loved this book. It is filled with so many snippets and gems of inspiration, love, hope and possibilities. I also love the way it's broken down into everyday thoughts helping all of us better our best in all we do. I especially enjoy your writing as it reminds me of the book I just co-authored with my granddaughter titled "Keeping Hearts Fed" with expressions to stimulate minds, encourage the imagination and feed hearts through this wonderful journey of life. I will cherish my copy." *TR Johnson Author & Entrepreneur www.the8snippets.com*

When editing for days or weeks at a stretch, my computer sometimes goes batty. Most of the time "refreshing" or "restarting" will correct the glitches. Annette Kingsley's book "Mindful Wisdom" is like the "refresher" button for humans. It is a chance to take a moment to re-set. I will be keeping a copy next to my computer, so that when I have a glitch or a crash, I can "refresh" and "restart." Thank you Annette for putting peace of mind in a book." - *Yuriko Gamo Romer, Film Maker, Flying Carp Productions www.flyingcarp.net*

Everyday Book of Insights is the kind of book I like to keep within arm's reach. Every page has something of value, something to read and then read again. My suggestion: Have two copies on hand, so you never have to give your own copy away or have your copy 'borrowed,' as mine was --and by my best friend!" - *Tom Callos, Martial Arts Business and Marketing Teacher, Curriculum Designer and Community Activist www.tomcallos.com*

"Be, Do, Have.... If you want clean teeth, brush them every day, if you want to be inspired, read - do something inspirational each and every day. Everyday Book of Insights is one of those tools that is a "must have" in your arsenal for personal growth and an inspirational teaching tool for anyone who educates children." - *Jon Jepson, 7th Degree, jjbbaGroup www.martialartsnottingham.com*

Annette Kingsley's Everyday Book of Insights is a beautiful piece of reading. I can feel my joy growing as the words lift me, just my style, one that I'll be able to come back year to year and see what words of wisdom that I deserve to hear that time around. I love a book that I can open to any page and receive its gifts. There are gems of truth that I can read with my daughters too, this is the legacy I want to pass onto my girls so that they'll always know...that they have a purpose in this life and their light shines! Thank you Annette." *-Tammi Putnam, Founder www.LawofAttraction123.com*

"I dipped in here and there as the feeling took me and using 'bibliomancy' I always found what was pertninent to my day, my moment, my being. Words can be beautiful things woven through pages like moments in our lives and in Annette Kingsley's book there are plenty of beautiful moments described on pages using woven words of wisdom, knowledge and hard won experience. Read it." *Chris Gill, Founder CFE Worldwide - Education, Coaching, Training and Consultancy www.cfeworldwide.com*

"I have read this over and over again and still get so many things from it. It reminds me of the way I continually read the Book of Five Rings, it is not something that you can ever finish but need and want to reference whenever you need to refocus and remember the way back onto your path! This book will be one of the books, that I personally will return to and reference in my classes. Thank you Annette Kingsley." *Grand Master Charles Ehrentraut - American Hapkido Martial Arts and Fitness, www.AmericanHapkidoCt.com*

I like the Everyday Book of Insights very much, I found it simple and complex at the same time, it's possible to read it on different levels and take what you want. A great mix of all of the best bits of information I have read and use, like a great reminder, yet at the same time expanding my understanding. It's definitely a book I will keep coming back to you and highly recommend." - Mark Gibbs, Entrepreneur & Teacher, www.climatecaregloabal.com

"I found it difficult to put down and make myself get some sleep as I just wanted to keep on reading! It's a real page turner."- *Jane Hubbard, Fashion Designer & Entrepreneur www.fairforme.com*

Contents

Foreword 3

Preface. 4

One. 8

Is Our Imagination Unleashed? 9

Need A Reason? 10

Mountains. 12

The Way. 13

Ok! 14

Empty Your Cup. 15

Don't Sweat It! 16

Energy. 17

A Simple List. 18

Adjusting. 20

Castles In The Air. 21

Simply By Sitting. 22

Transition. 23

Unique. 24

Only Today. 25

Like It Or Not? 26

1, 3 or 20? 28

Excellence 32

Reap What We Sow. 33

Limited? 34

Delighted. 36

You Know Don't You? 37

Balancing Act. 38

Wishing Well. 40

Sunshine. 41

In a Snap. 42

How Much Do You Value Your Time? 44

Enlightenment. 45

Purpose Belief Inspiration Action 47

Heart Or Head? 48

Is It A Nightmare? 49

One More Time. 50

Will. 52

You Are Great Already. 54

Do More. 56

What Are You Thinking About? 58

Flow Around Obstacles. 60

Keep The Faith. 61

Mistakes Are The Business. 62

Questions? 64

Doing. 65

A Year Planner? 66

Genius. 68

Individuality. 69

A Suitable Path? 70

Gesture. 71

Is There Anything Else Out There? 72

Roller Coaster.	74
Purpose, Vision & Goals.	75
Is Your Character Yours?	76
Give Up?	78
Super Strong Diversity.	79
Do You Have A Pet?	80
Begin.	81
Time For Tea? (or Coffee).	82
Decisions, Decisions?	84
Let's Pretend.	86
Give Away Riches.	87
Did You Get What You Wanted?	88
Priority.	90
On Time Or Late?	92
Today.	94
Keep on Walking.	95
When Will Wisdom Come?	96
Calm.	97
Are We There Yet?	98
The Art Of Balance.	99
Imagine.	100
Enough Courage?	102
Whole Health.	103
Who Cares?	104
Possibility.	105
Stick With Your Ideas.	106

Our Earth.	107
Comfortable?	108
Partial.	109
Growth.	110
The Point Is?	111
Dreamers.	112
Admiration.	114
Circumstances.	116
Acres Of Diamonds.	118
Carefree.	120
Concentrate.	122
A Combined Harmony.	123
Have You Found It Yet?	124
What To Do?	126
Empty & Full.	128
Pass The Buck?	130
Poverty & Want	131
Are You Lucky?	132
Moving On To Higher Ground.	134
Stepping Stones.	135
Afraid Of The Dark?	136
Your Greatest Enemy.	137
Colourful.	138
Woolgathering Is It A Good Thing?	139
Definitive List.	140
Chaos Or Order?	142

Be Very Weary Of The Word 'Lack'.	143
Recycle.	144
Rain.	146
A True Friend.	147
Beautiful.	148
Are You A Big Shot Or A Little One?	149
Peace To All.	150
Are You Secretly Happy?	151
Could You Cry?	152
Miracle.	153
Grace.	154
Touch The Earth.	155
Are You Your Own Master?	156
Back To The Start.	157
True to Yourself.	158
Begins In.	159
Humorous?	162
Yes You Can.	163
Window Of Opportunity.	164
This Is The End?	165
Abundance.	166
News.	168
Not Just Yet.	169
Is It Fear Of Failure Or Feedback?	170
Can You See Past The Clutter?	172
Repetition Is The Mother Of All Skill.	175

Honesty.	176
Wu Wei.	177
Are You Feeling Grateful Today?	178
Are You A Pessimist, Optimist Or Realist?	180
Your Favourite Colour?	181
Your Repertoire.	182
Second Thoughts?	184
It's Time.	186
Lost In Translation.	188
How Strong Are You Feeling Today?	190
Too Old To Learn?	193
The Eternal Quest.	194
Care To The End.	196
Nothing.	197
Thank-you.	198
Index.	200
You Are Cordially Invited.	209

"Whatever you do, or dream you can, begin it.

Boldness has genius and power and magic in it."

- Johann Wolfgang von Goethe

Everyday Book of Insights

Foreword.

This gem of a book is an absolute must read for anyone walking the path of spiritual, personal development and self mastery.

Brimming full of "enlightening" philosophy, sound advice and practical tips, Everday Book of Insights reminds us that we create our own reality and that the creative power we all have "within" is the primary cause of our effects.

This includes the effects on our health, happiness, finances, relationships, or anything else we might choose to "intentionally" be, do or have.

Throughout the book, Annette Kingsley guides you gently along the path to living your life as you would love it to be, with passion and deliberation but also with the courage and determination to really see it through.

Everday Book of Insights is a joy to read and offers you the keys to unlock the shackles that bind so many to a life of struggle and mediocrity.

The more you awaken to the universal truths revealed within these pages the more you will be empowered to create positive change and gracefully ease forward into the life of your dreams.

Annette Kingsley reminds us beautifully that we are not powerless we are powerful – So read on and enjoy – you'll be glad you did.

Darren Pugh, creativewarriortraining.com

Preface.

To truly live a happy, healthy life; blessed with love, purpose, balance and passion and to feel complete and fulfilled takes some doing. Like anything worth obtaining in this lifetime it requires some dedication, effort and resolve.

First it takes the decision that you are going to take the time to invest in yourself comprehensively and that you absolutely want to expand, evolve and engage with your inner self more. Those that chose to not take this path can often times find themselves being held captive, under the lock and key of their own mind.

We however, are on a mission, an unavoidable magnetic pull in to the unknown, a life of sensational adventure, sometimes gritty adversity and spectacular moments of bliss. It will always deliver on being engaging and challenging and be one that requires a good healthy dash of indomitable spirit to reach that pinnacle, whatever or wherever it might be.

There are extraordinary amounts of genius, possibilities and compassion; opportunities of far-reaching friendships, mind boggling inventions, ideas, art and science and more, all of which can be truly breathtaking if only they are let out in to the world. Many of those that were once a single thought, we now see around us today and others we can observe through our human history; there are undoubtedly even things we might not yet know about ourselves, if only we all dare to do something with our dreams.

Along the way you realise that the end is not somewhere outside of you, it's the start on the inside. However a few meditations, affirmations and happy beads aren't going to fool your subconscious mind that this is 'it' because 'it' isn't even a tangible idea to begin with. This utopia can only be found though a combined harmony of the whole self and not just a small aspect of it. We all actually have to work diligently on this for our whole lives and not just a fleeting moment of it; which of course for many is a real joy but for others is an implausible notion.

Our mind is a central theme which we are forever compelled towards in our quest for advancement, harmony and accomplishment; it is our control centre and combined with our heart and intuition is ultimately going to govern our unique outcomes in life. With the current information from neuroscience, psychology and personal development coupled with our traditional wisdom and philosophies dating back several thousands of years we find ourselves in an extremely wonderful place of choice and of deliberate mental creation. Accompanied with mentoring and support systems to ensure we find our optimum selves and capabilities long before we quit and give up, feeling alone, despondent and quite possibly for some of us with a peppering of self sabotage along the way.

My fellow travelers we have but two choices it seems; to throw our arms open wide, to take in a big deep breath and throw out all former nonsensical beliefs, non serving information and any other clutter that is clouding our minds and to consciously walk forward mindfully day by day. To stop and be present and allow ourselves the moments to take in all that is the wonder of Mother Nature and our scintillating Earth; to share, love, laugh and learn, to stop and be kind to others and yourself. To make a true commitment to yourself that you will not sell yourself short, that you will never ever give up or give in during this life time and that you will do your absolute best, no matter what shall pass on by as you go.

You have purpose already inside of you and naturally are an embodiment of happiness if you allow it; you will find your way, regardless of where you are right now, or where you have come from. The alternative is of course to carry on regardless, to ignore any life lessons, not invest in yourself and to shrug your shoulders and think "this is it, what it's always been and always will be". This cruel game of the mind can be dispensed with at will but you have to consciously want it to be. As amazing as it is already your mind will not change for the better without the nod from you, the controller at its helm.

It is to those then, that seek their bigger, better self, the path of service and purpose and greater findings within that this book is written for. The ongoing premise of this books creation was to garner a collection of notes which have evolved out of the work from my many years of teaching within the Martial Arts, business, personal development and writing; and most recently through my blog - mindful wisdom (although these particular notes are in this book only) and its predecessor black belt thinking (and their respective Facebook pages), to enable you to be able to seek them at will.

Most of us benefit from a daily 'hit' of motivation and inspiration and we can only gain a positive overtone from being coached, nudged or pushed along at times as it's our human nature to be our most dazzling when we are interdependent and the smartest way we can truly take flight in to realms the future has yet to yield to us.

You can read this book in the order it comes; you can randomly pick a note when the mood takes you or search for a particular topic of interest. But whatever you do, make a deliberate choice today to foster a resolute stand for you, to commit to creating an ongoing balanced, fulfilled and happy life, one where you are challenged, energized and living the bliss that you were always meant to.

Here's to your success in whatever sense of the word engages you and to your abundant, balanced and colourful life.

One.

There is only one you, one day that is today and one lifetime like this one. So with your one you can join with others and create the best life you deserve, you dream of and you know in your heart is possible.

Choose your friends, business partners, and co-creators carefully and deliberately because you've probably noticed that when everything is right, it just 'is' and you can instinctively feel it. Alas when it's not and things are awry then nothing falls in to place as it should do.

You maybe one but you are all that is needed to make your indelible mark on this planet - you just have to decide what that might be.

Think carefully, make those decisions and take some serious action. There's a whole lifetime to make all your dreams come true. But start you must.

> "Somebody should tell us, right at the start of our lives, that we are dying. Then we might live life to the limit, every minute of every day. Do it! I say. Whatever you want to do, do it now! There are only so many tomorrows." - Michael Landon

Is Our Imagination Unleashed?

"Nothing limits achievement like small thinking; nothing expands possibilities like unleashed imagination." - William Arthur Ward

A note to any naysayers in your life. Remember their small thinking is why they want yours to be, their fears for your safety are their own, their reigns are pulling you in, so they don't have to step outside their comfort zones.

If you un-tether yourself from everyone and be truly free to let your imagination be, do or have whatever it likes, then you will find yourself in places that you dreamed of because that's where your dreams and your imagination reside.

Be free my friend and fly to wherever takes your fancy. Don't look back or look down, don't doubt yourself and just believe wholeheartedly in yourself.

Need A Reason?

Sometimes people need a reason, a purpose or a push to get started.

The reason(s) can be anything, simple gestures to life changing jaw dropping events and circumstances that seem to descend upon you from somewhere or nowhere

When you think about it, the reason already happened. It came here in the first breath you took when you arrived on planet Earth.

It was there through your first few hours of life and it has been there ever since, slowly ticking away in the back ground.

For you and everyone around you, is a walking, talking, ticking clock, going somewhere for some reason.

We arrive in all shapes and sizes, tones and personalities. We share and disagree on so much and so little.

You began your life with everything in a compact case.

You might be loud or soft, bold or demure.

You could be bursting with so much to say or quiet with contemplation and reflection.

None the less. You had your reason already.

You arrived.

Don't wait until it's too late and the battery is going flat, for your clock won't tick forever.

You are the reason. Make your time count.

> "If we do not believe within ourselves this deeply rooted feeling that there is something higher than ourselves, we shall never find the strength to evolve into something higher." Rudolf Steiner

Mountains.

The Peak-

A mountain of hope

Or a mountain to climb?

A long walk to see what's on the other side.

Or stay home, don't bother and sit and wonder what if?

A mountain top vista is a beautiful site to see, feel and breathe

But the same can be said from viewing the range from the ground

You can choose to be up or you can choose to be down, it's your choice

It can be getting better every day in every way or it can be a living nightmare

You can paint your mountains the way you like, or search for a gorgeous picture

Take a deep breath and know another day will come; another idea will likely spring,

Someone somewhere will help you and someone loves you too, no matter what happens.

I hope you like this little mountain we have just created, the Universe is full of them.

The Way.

The Way is your way.

The Way is the only way.

The Way is a single step.

The Way is a wave of happiness.

Or a single tear.

The Way can be ignored, tested or disliked, it won't mind.

Because ultimately the Way was there all along and will be there for ever more.

The Way. It's a choice; a way of life.

A new direction. An old friend.

And by the way, it will always be there for you so don't worry about losing it, for it will find you easily enough.

Just remember there is no set way, your way is perfect enough for you.

> "The way of the superior person is threefold; virtuous, they are free from anxieties; wise they are free from perplexities; and bold they are free from fear." - Confucius

Okay!

It's okay if things aren't perfect.

It's okay if you forget.

It's okay if today isn't going as planned.

It's okay to change your mind.

It's okay to wonder if you are doing the right thing.

It's okay to just laugh it off.

It's okay to take 5 and do nothing.

It's okay when sometimes you can't be bothered.

It's okay if you are super enthusiastic when no-one else is.

It's okay if others don't see it like you do.

It's okay to be fantastic at one thing and pretty bad at something else.

It's okay because you are more than okay; you are exceptional.

You do so much already.

Don't worry about the tiny, little things or even something giant.

In the grand scheme of things. It's all just - a okay.

Empty Your Cup.

The Zen master Nan-in during the Meiji era received a visit from university professor.

Nan-in served tea and poured it until his visitor's cup became full and kept on pouring, until it spilled all over the table.

The professor watched the overflow until he could no longer restrain himself. "Stop, it's overfull, no more will go in!"

"And you" continued Nan-in, "are you to full of your own opinions? How can you learn when first you must empty your cup." - Zen Koan

We are all too full of many opinions, even though some maybe be sound, true or reasonably accurate.

Once in a while we must let it go and flow with the wind to rest upon something new.

And in the newness we become renewed, our inner child can be happy.

For our curiosity and seeking comes with us when we are born and stays with us all the way to the end but where the end is exactly no-one really knows.

So just keep on filling and emptying your cup and enjoy the moment for the purity and greatness of what it is.

Don't Sweat It!

Have you ever noticed how it is easy to nod you head in agreement at the phrase 'Don't sweat the small stuff' but in the thick of it all, in the heat of the moment, at the time when a particular experience is a reality to you, it is much harder to do?

Like most of our habits, beliefs and thought processes - they are learned, installed by others, taught in schools, acquired somewhere along the lines of our growing up.

As a grown up we have to decide - are we going to make life easier for ourselves or harder?

Do you think you have enough 'stuff' being thrown at you by life and others as it is?

If so, next time you find yourself caught up in one of those little tizzies - smile, breathe and say 'you know what, it's not worth it' in the grand scheme of the Universe this is a minor event.

Move on, our time is far too short and way too precious for this triviality that engulfs us.

Let's be strong, let's be bold, let's get out of here.

Next.

> "To know and to act are one and the same" - Samurai Maxim

Energy.

"Energy flows where attention goes!" - Michael Beckwith

Energy is everything and everything is energy.

That said, you can be bright positive energy or dark negative energy or even something in between.

Our natural universal yin yang will push and pull us back and forth.

But you can be conscious of the energy you are omitting and if you don't like it, change it. Or at the very least be mindful of it.

Simple to say, not so simple to do? Well that depends on how much you are actually enjoying the moaning, sulking, being down or other. Sometimes we seem to think that serves us, sometimes it doesn't.

We are human so let us be that which we choose to be.

Just remember that it is you that gets to make that choice and not someone else.

Otherwise, it's their energy controlling yours and that is just a hi-jack of your good energy.

Best take it back then.

A Simple List.

Have you ever considered what a faithful friend 'the list' is?

It's a reminder.

It's a help you focus kind of thing.

It helps you get things done in order of priority.

It doesn't forget, even if you do.

It won't judge you, if you scribble all over it and change your mind.

It won't ever leave you.

It is dependable.

And you confide in it.

Maybe seeing how special it is, we should treat it a little better?

Perhaps we could have a smart book or a personal journal or similar to write it in?

We could maybe have a special pen to write it with?

We could perhaps spend a little more time with it?

Really we should see it as the start of a very special relationship, for it is truly committed to our improvement and evolvement, it can take us any place we like, if we stick to it's rules.

Rules? What rules?

Think carefully about what we write on it.

Decide purposefully on what the list contains.

Look at it regularly.

Update it frequently.

And don't forget to tick it off with glee when we complete a task.

Then when we come to change it and make a new one we shall celebrate our victories, for no matter how small they are leading us to a mighty crescendo somewhere down the line.

Yippee, you are allowed to be happy, dance and jump about or sit quietly with a cup of tea and smile, whichever you prefer.

The fact is, you and your list are going places...

The hard part is deciding where?

Adjusting.

Taking constant tiny, medium and large sized adjustments are the difference between you being on the brink of 'success' or in the lap of 'failure'.

Too often people give up or say something can't be done.

In actual fact, they should take responsibility and admit they cannot be bothered to try.

For when you really, really, absolutely, passionately want to achieve something or complete anything you totally, utterly and dependably will find a way.

Remember even a little millimetre each day after a year would chart a totally different destination on a map and so in your life.

So don't give up, adjust away instead.

> **"When it is obvious that the goals cannot be reached, don't adjust the goals, adjust the action steps."** - Confucius

Castles In The Air...

> "Do not worry if you have built your castles in the air. They are where they should be. Now put the foundations under them." Henry David Thoreau

Not enough is said about foundations is there? Too much emphasis is put on the 'results' and how quick you can get them.

Sometimes our seemingly floppy culture is so because we allow it to be centered on having it all right now, at any price or in any way, regardless of whether we want it that way or not.

In fact most people haven't a clue. It's a frenzied sale day, grabbing anything at a 'bargain price'; only later do you look back and think 'what did I buy that for'?

Your deepest, inner most dreams and aspirations aren't bargains. The Universe didn't invest it's best in you to be sold for peanuts.

I'm afraid you're like an antique, you are going to get better with age as you gain more history. As each decade passes something more has been added on to your life's journey.

And foundations only last when they are built as so, just as they are indeed intended to.

Cheap and flimsy you are not.

Solid and regal you are.

Roll your sleeves up then, you're in this for the long haul.

Simply By Sitting.

"Sometimes, simply by sitting, the soul collects wisdom." - Zen Proverb

When was the last time you spent several minutes sitting in silence? None of us probably do this enough. In this case silence equals:-

No phones / mobiles / texts / bleeps & alerts going off.

No social media or the internet - full stop.

No TV / radio / audio / podcasts etc.

No background noise.

No-one else talking to you or at you.

Sorry but no children either - that is shouting, screaming, playing, laughing or crying.

No animals wanting feeding / going out or whatever else.

Anything else that makes a noise and distracts you.

So peace and quiet is unadulterated silence.

Calmness, stillness, deep breathing, being at one.

Now we are getting somewhere and we wonder why we don't take things in or remember much.

Is there anything in this do you think? Try it and see.

Transition.

When something is difficult or challenging in life, it might help to view it as a 'transitional' phase.

That is; we are moving through one episode of our life's movie in to another one.

Sometimes things are going be tough, unpleasant, uncomfortable and so on.

But you know already don't you, that you will make it through, you will see the other side?

Just make the decision to consciously accept this is a transitional phase and say 'I will get through this'.

Smile and relax. The Universe is supporting you.

These things that test us, often serve us and put more muscle on to us, they toughen us up and enable us to cope with even bigger aspects of the life we are moving towards.

We wouldn't expect a seed to sprout and grow and be a huge tree in the morning now would we? So how can we expect ourselves to be?

Transitions are good. You are moving forward. Progress is happening, it is here.

Tomorrow you will awake that one step closer, braver and stronger and that's a good thing isn't it?

Unique.

As there is only one of you, ever, here on this Earth.

You might remember to cut yourself some slack, give your self some praise and know you are here for your reasons, you are encouraged to be your true self and to let your light shine out of you.

You *are* a shining star, make the most of it because the Universe is going to call you back in to the night stars one day but until then, shine, shine, shine.

Only Today.

"Yesterday is ashes; tomorrow wood.

Only today does the fire burn brightly." - Inuit Proverb

Today counts.

So make it happen.

What can you do?

What goals can you set?

What small step could you take?

Who could you speak to?

What could you research?

What could you read or listen to?

How can you turn your dreams in to reality?

Only today can you make it happen.

Like It Or Not?

Sometimes it can seem that you are dealt something that you could really do without.

Have you ever received any news, e-mail or a phone call where you thought, "you are joking, not now?"

You could be forgiven for sometimes looking up to the heaven's and thinking why me, why now?

When you give it some real thought however, is there ever a good time for a challenge?

When is it convenient to have to deal with these things?

If you have children, is there ever the 'right' and 'perfect' time for that?

Is it just the right time to do something new, try a new venture or to shout, 'hold on I'm going in'!

Probably not.

What we would probably be better remembering is that we are all a part of the Universe, mini extensions of it and fortunate enough to be experiencing our very own expression of our Way.

If you have good health, then the more you have to celebrate.

Sometimes, whether we like it or not we are dealt a hand that really could be the making of us. It could be the time we step up, the time we change our attitude, the moment where we rise above it all, a moment in time where we think, enough is enough.

So rather than dwell on the inconvenience, we should spend our time relishing the new challenge. The Tao clearly thinks we are up to the job and that we will 'cope' and get through it - one way or another because of course we are all part of the Oneness and can.

The more self mastery you have over your emotions, attitude, actions and decisions, the more you will deal with the situation appropriately and be in tune with your Universal Self.

So see it as like a belt test in the Martial Arts or some other test in life, business or sport where you will be graduating on to the next level.

Ultimately the choices you make right now will yield the crop of what you will become tomorrow.

1, 3 or 20?

Depending on what statistic you use, around the world today approximately 1% minimum to 20% maximum are the amount of people who set goals and follow them up.

Let's just detail what that entails.

That is:

Phase 1. Sitting down and thinking

Phase 2. Actually writing out goals.

Phase 3. Looking at them daily, re-writing them out, speaking them aloud.

Phase 4. Discussing those goals with other people.

Phase 5. Doing any necessary research on those goals.

Phase 6. Doing daily small steps on any given goal.

Phase 7. Reviewing the progress of the goals.

Phase 8. Adjusting, changing, deleting, re-defining any of the goals.

Phase 9. Reviewing current progress.

Phase 10. Never quitting, giving up or forgetting about the goals.

Phase 11. Taking further inspired daily action.

Phase 12. Accepting any 'failures' as feedback.

Phase 13. Starting the process over.

Phase 14. Repeat

As you can see from that list, some of the basic but fundamental elements will lose most people, maybe even you at times?

Some will argue they are busy, they have commitments, families and so on.

Of course, this is true but no-one can argue that if you don't take full responsibility for your actions, thoughts and results, then whatever you get is going to be in the lap of the Gods or worse still other people.

The list may seem a little exhausting. But picture this...

Your conscious brain sits down to write out a goal list and thinks 'I don't really have the time for this', 'I can't be bothered right now I'm tired', but 'I do want x though'

Okay over to the sub-conscious brain receiving the messages and instructions from it's conscious counter part.

Okay today's plan is?

No time

Can't be bothered

Wanting

'Fabulous, an easy day for me then','I don't have to do anything at all', 'Nice'

Back to the control room.

Wants stay wants.

Tiredness & Lack of time will always be there and so no worries about that.

So let's re-write that.

Take the time to instruct yourself in the manner that you actually would like to receive them in.

Ensure that your sub-conscious mind is filled with positive, can-do attitude and action points.

Do not worry about the how's and the details, the Universe will fill in the way and specifics another day.

Concentrate 100% of your effort and attention on creating the plan and then nibbling away a little each day on the lettuce leaf.

Little by little, step by step the dots will start joining together.

It will take time and yes you might need to rub out a few of the drawings along the way.

But eventually you will get there and you will complete that particular set of goals, one way or another and each will transform in to whatever they are meant to be - that is between the Universe and you.

But as they say 'you've got to be in it to win it'.

So are you in it?

Be part of the magical small percentage not the masses still yawning, moaning and wondering where it all went wrong.

Excellence.

At times we say we are in 'search' of excellence but really it's there all along.

It's there when you do what you don't feel like doing, it's there when you are in despair but get up anyway, it's there at your lowest moments and it's there when you feel real joy.

Excellence isn't something we should be looking for, humbly speaking it is what we are working towards every day.

You then already are most excellent and to the degree will depend upon your commitment, dedication and self discipline.

But what are the other options?

What do you think they are?

Which route you take is up to you.

But to try your optimum best is always the best policy.

> "The price of excellence is discipline. The cost of mediocrity is disappointment." - William Athur Ward

Reap What We Sow.

Today take a look at your collective gardens and take time to consider them, each individually.

The garden of your mind, your body and spirit and the one that you may have around your home.

You know that if you think, plan and prepare, take consistent action and habitually are doing the best you can that somewhere down the road you will find copious blooms, seasonal delights and fragrances from the heavens.

So this week take stock and make some time to think about what you eat, how you live, what you say and do and how you expect your outcomes to be.

If you don't put the best in to yourself how can you get the best out of yourself? You are worth the effort, so aim for your most excellent effort as often as you can and see what results that produces.

Happy gardening.

Limited?

The word 'limited' looks contained, all purse lipped and tight looking, doesn't it?

When you ask yourself 'how' you can be, do or have whatever it maybe. Your mind instantly opens up because how is a question and that single expansion in thought will allow you to be open to answers, possibilities and solutions.

Conversely, if you say 'can't' or 'won't' then of course as you know that is true already because you have closed off your mind to any other possible outcome, regardless of whether there was an alternative on hand.

Transformational vocabulary might sound a bit woolly but in fact it's strength lies in the meaning of the altered word(s) such as:-

Small thinking - HUGE thinking

Limited - U-n-l-i-m-i-t-e-d

Tethered - Unleashed

Failure - Achievement

Can't - Can or How?

Won't - WILL

Thoughtless - I-m-a-g-i-n-a-t-i-o-n

Small - E x p a n s i o n

No - Yes!

Give it a whirl today and see what you come up with and see what you can or should replace in your own vocabulary.

A small word can make a massive difference. Yes?

> "Your time is limited, so don't waste it living someone else's life. Don't be trapped by dogma - which is living with the results of other people's thinking. Don't let the noise of other's opinions drown out your own inner voice. And most important, have the courage to follow your heart and intuition. They somehow already know what you truly want to become. Everything else is secondary." - Steve Jobs

Delighted.

Are you delighted today?

Well you should be. You are alive and kicking, breathing and thinking aren't you?

You have a whole new fresh day ahead.

If you don't like the word delighted much how about one of these alternatives?

captivated, charmed, ecstatic, elated, enchanted, entranced, excited, fulfilled, gladdened, gratified, joyous, jubilant, overjoyed, pleasantly surprised, pleased, thrilled.....

Find one you like and apply it to your day and see what happens.

You can't help but smile can you?

You Know Don't You?

You have always known and you will continue to know. The trick is to tap in to it and keep the source open, it will flow freely when the time is right and guard you against when the time is not.

Have faith and belief in yourself above all else at all times. It will not fail you, it will support, guide and lead you beautifully forward.

> "At the centre of your being you have the answer; you know who you are and you know what you want." - Lao Tzu

Balancing Act.

Life is a constant *balancing* act.

There is no secret method.

It can't be rushed.

And it takes time to perfect.

You have to work with it.

And you have to want to do it.

But like a tight rope walker you can get better day by day.

You have to be clear what it is you are actually balancing.

Then you want to have a strong idea about the time frames involved.

You will need to decide what sections of projects, tasks, goals and commitments you want to include. And how much time you will assign to each of them.

You can take a very simple approach such as dividing your day in to morning, afternoon and evening. Or you can take blocks of hours and divide them up that way.

But without taking the time out to do the process you will have no real answer in how you currently divide your time.

Time can go so fast and can be consumed by small things that end up taking big chunks out of your day.

You may be overwhelmed at times by too much to do and so many demands. Or you might even be under whelmed if the 'to do list' isn't that inspiring to you.

You have to get tough, you have to weed out the debris and clear the clutter.

You need to take responsibility and take control.

You are the one in the director's chair and it's your voice you answer to.

The art of balance is worth the effort. For it's rewards are fulfillment, contentment, satisfaction, harmony and happiness.

So take out a sheet of paper and write down what you want to spend your time doing and how much time you want to spend doing each of the items on your list.

Divide this up however best suits you and take notes all week long to see how you do.

You might be surprised at those little 'leaks' of time, which will give you the opportunity to plug them up!

And you could even find something on there you want to erase and something else that you want to expand.

There is no secret to balance as such except the secret that those who do can gain it and those who don't, well they have no clue because they didn't look for it.

Wishing Well.

Have you ever thrown a coin in to a wishing well and well, wished?

Some days do you wish for something that has happened or wish something hadn't?

Wishing is a bit wishy washy though isn't it?

It's a bit of an empty air head.

You can of course 'wish' someone well or a Happy Birthday but even then it's bit wobbly.

Turn your wishes in to something more concrete or dissolve them clean away.

In the case of the past, don't waste time wishing it didn't happen, just glean from the experience the best you can and move on, leaving it behind, where it's best left.

In the case of the future, don't wish for something, get it out of your head, on to paper or with pictures and go get it by gradually moving towards it and the way will present itself.

Little by little you can turn those wishy washy wishes in to gigantic goals that you can grasp and do away with those mundane and meaningless words that aren't doing you any favours.

Sunshine.

Most of us are happier in the sunshine and some can constantly seek the weather forecast to help us evaluate whether today will be a good day or not.

Some of us are able to have humour at our most darkest moments.

Some people are able to laugh no matter what.

Whether it be the kind of sunshine you see or you feel, one thing can be certain.

You are the both the giver and receiver of sunshine and whether you let it in or let it out, is all down to you.

Fancy a little sunshine today?

> **"A good laugh is sunshine in the house." - William Makepeace Thackeray**

In a Snap.

How many times have you made a snap decision?

Do you rely on this to make your decisions?

Does the decision come from your intuition at lightning speeds or your processing brain?

Highly likely the faster we decide the more intuitive it is.

When we think about something, we start weighing things up, reading, researching, listening and so on. Yes, we might be making a 'considered' or 'informed choice' and the likes but really we have already made our mind up.

Usually, we already know whether we want to do something or want something or not or whether we would like to go somewhere, or maybe meet someone or not.

Regardless of whether you can, in terms of time, money, circumstance and similar. The vast majority of us can make a decision in a snap.

Yes, there might be times where you later live to 'regret' some decisions, or wonder what an earth your were thinking but that's all part and parcel of life's intricate tapestry weaving away.

The yin and the yang, typically balances itself out.

We can't expect every decision we make to be 100% perfect, robust and unquestionable now can we?

On the flip side, believe in yourself, your decisions, your snappy little thoughts, they are right at the time for a reason, a lesson, an experience or a step towards something else that you haven't quite met yet.

So keep practising those little snappy snaps and you'll just keep getting beautifully better.

How Much Do You Value Your Time?

It is imperative that you address what you are using your time for so you can deduce if any of it is being wasted. That is, do you say yes when you mean no? Do you feel pushed, pressured or usurped in to doing something you would rather not? Are you spending too much time on the things you least enjoy and not enough time on what you most enjoy?

Every day, week or month, just take a review of your diary, organiser or however you keep track of what you are doing. If you do not at present start now and grab a journal or a diary and get started.

Can you see any patterns? Do you start the day, week or month off well and then s-l-i-d-e…? Do you end up not crossing off your list and instead doing someone else's?

By just being mindful of your time is a good start or place to end up. From there you can make improvements and revisions. The best part is that you just keep on making those small incremental changes until you are 100% happy with what you are doing on a daily basis - yes this may take some time. But the other choice is to stay stuck and not make any improvement?

A side note to parents and busy people: Of course some of our day is given over to others and some of our time maybe spent helping others, being a chauffeur (mums and dads), lending an ear to a friend, replying to e-mail and so on.

Providing you are happy with all of those elements then that is a given so it is the *rest* of your time we are talking about.

Of course, if you are unhappy with for example someone calling you up week in week out and down loading their stuff on to your shoulders - then you are going to have to make a decision; you either speak up or put up with it; does this serve you or your friend? Alternatively find a way to peeter-out this unresourceful use of your time for example.

Essentially you have to take a look and decide how you divide your time up and between whom you are going to give a percentage of that time too. Stressed out people or parents are allowed to take a break, so allow yourself one.

> "Time is the coin of your life. It is the only coin you have, and only you can determine how it will be spent. Be careful lest you let other people spend it for you."
> Carl Sandburg

Enlightenment.

Some seek it.

Some find it.

Some don't care.

Is it illusive?

Can it be ambiguous?

Who knows?

Whose known all along?

Already you are wise, you know more than you might even know you know.

> "It is nonsense to insist that we cannot achieve enlightenment without learned and pious teachers.
>
> Because wisdom is innate, we can all enlighten ourselves." - Hui Neng

Purpose Belief Inspiration Action

Simple steps to abundance, balance and happiness.

Have a purpose. Find your point, reason, values and ambitions.

Maintain rock solid belief in yourself and the way will come to you.

Give yourself continuous inspiration to fuel your motivation.

Take small or large daily action steps forever moving forward.

No magic spells or wands are used in this recipe.

It is just about you and your continued perseverance in tackling these steps every day and week regardless of whether you 'feel' like it or not.

If you want a reminder, have your very own purpose belief inspiration action mug, t-shirt or journal to help inspire you and keep you on task.

> "If Heaven made him - earth can find some use for him."
> - Chinese Proverb

http://www.cafepress.co.uk/mindfulwisdom

Heart Or Head?

"Follow your heart during your lifetime; do not do more than what is commanded you." - Ancient Egyptian Wisdom

Follow both your heart and your head in that order.

Your heart will yield your loves and bliss, your head will help you get there.

Your intuition will help keep you on your correct path.

And your combined ability of knowing and feeling what is right with your copious amounts of wisdom both owned, learned already and not yet seen will see you through.

Your life's most truthful path is awaiting you up ahead just stick to your own and let other's travel theirs.

Is It A Nightmare?

"Vision without action is a daydream. Action without vision is a nightmare." - Japanese Proverb

A mantra for the masses.

To not have any vision, any goals and to not take action is at best, a mindless existence.

But to live your daydreams, to create your vision and to take just one small step each day, transcends the nightmare in to a beautiful living harmony.

Let's dream, let us be mindful, let us choose to take action.

Then people might say, 'we're living the dream' because we are, aren't we?"

One More Time.

Have you ever thought to yourself - "I just can't carry on", or "I've had enough of this", or "It's no use it's just not working / going to happen" and so on?

We read lots of motivational quotes and sayings, that say you should never give up. Success is just around the corner. Never quit you will get there in the end.

Whilst that is highly probable to one degree or another.

How do you actually hang in there? Have you ever thought "How am I going to get through this?"

And how did you get through it? What did you do? Who did you speak to? What did you read or listen to or watch maybe? Have you written it down?

If you have then that is truly fantastic. If you haven't then you are like most people in that we don't really consider these things until we are descended in to the thick of it. By then it might be too late and some people will just give up. They have no back up, no help or clue what to do. So they freeze and withdraw.

What could be highly beneficial to us, is if we consider when we are in a fabulous mood, if something not so good was to happen right now, what sort of cavalry would you call upon?

Do you want music or quiet time?

Is there somewhere special you like to visit or a particular person you would like to see?

Do you have a list of favourite quotes or books that help lift you or inspire you?

How about reading about other people that have gone through some transforming times and see what helped them through it by reading autobiographies and the likes.

It seems funny to think that most of us have a first aid kit of sorts when we have cuts and bruises and yet 'first-aid for the mind' isn't really considered. We wouldn't hesitate in seeing a doctor, having complementary medicine or holistic methods to help our bodies, yet when our minds really need some support, there is often no help or back up.

People seem to expect the mind to sort everything out pronto because our evidence has been that it usually can. However just like a Mercedes-benz or an Aston Martin no matter how great something might appear on a visual level at some point something will go wrong with it from a mechanical, physical or general aspect of it, that is normal.

So help yourself out, get yourself a 'one more time - first-aid for the mind kit' in order to give yourself a helping hand. You know your own mind better than anyone else so you know exactly what can help you and what can hinder you too. We all need some inspiration and new ideas so have a good think and see what you can come up with.

Will.

This is a sample of a dictionary definition of a person's 'will'. Not exhaustive but enough illustration for now...

Will

1. the faculty of conscious and especially of deliberate action; the power of control the mind has over its own actions: the freedom of the will.

2. power of choosing one's own actions: to have a strong or a weak will.

3. the act or process of using or asserting one's choice; volition: My hands are obedient to my will.

4. wish or desire: to submit against one's will.

5. purpose or determination, often hearty or stubborn determination; willfulness: to have the will to succeed.

6. the wish or purpose as carried out, or to be carried out: to work one's will.

7. disposition, whether good or ill, toward another.

The freedom of your will and the use of your will is a subject of great length, debate and of varying outcomes.

One thing is for sure, to be mindful of your will is advisable and to use your will with wisdom is essential.

The will on it's own can't really accomplish anything but your will set against the back drop of your self-discipline, courage, indomitable spirit, defined task or life's work will surely find itself challenged at times, maybe weakened at others but at the end of the day it's pretty unshakeable.

Your resolve to maintain a super strong force with your own free will combined with your plan of action and supporting team will always be a force to be reckoned with.

A quick flick through our history pages will show what the strength of will our forebears have had and the amazing achievements littered through the years have brought us.

Your will is as strong as you want it to be for it is a force from, of and within the Universe. There is no end as there is no end to the choices and parameters you have at your will.

> "The power of will is the supreme court over all other departments of my mind. I will exercise it daily when I need the urge to action for any purpose, and I will form habits designed to bring the power of my will into action at least once daily." - Bruce Lee

You Are Great Already.

The trick to 'being' great, is to believe you are already because actually you are.

You have everything you will ever need already inside you to be, do or have whatever it is you want to be, do or have.

What separates people is the knowing and believing. For example someone with lowered self esteem may dither on a decision, some one with a lack of self confidence may be unsure if anyone is really going to want to hear whatever it is they have to say.

The people that 'just do it', are really just the people who have decided it is better to try something and not succeed (the first time or the tenth) but to keep on going regardless; knowing that everything will work out in the end.

Because every time we take a step forward we learn something new, about ourselves, about whatever it is we are hoping to achieve and about other people and life itself.

Funnily enough the more you do, learn, grow and stretch yourself the better and easier these steps are to take.

Yes, you are allowed a down day or an off day but treat it as just that, not a monumental, colossal end of the world kind of thing.

So keep mindful of the fact you can and will find that which you need when it is time and just get going.

"We are unlimited beings. We have no ceiling. The capabilities and the talents and the gifts and the power that is within every single individual that is on this planet, is unlimited." - Michael Beckwith

Do More.

No matter how hard it is and it can be so hard at times to just get by for so many people, for so many reasons. It is understandable that sometimes we just can't seem to see the point or find the Way.

Remember these words for they are like plant food. Feed them, nurture them, water them and watch them grow. Dig deep when you have to but just keep going no matter what. Just do not stop. Ever.

> "Do more than belong: participate. Do more than care: help. Do more than believe: practice. Do more than be fair: be kind. Do more than forgive: forget. Do more than dream: work." William Arthur Ward

Is The Time Ever Right?

"Do not wait; the time will never be "just right." Start where you stand, and work with whatever tools you may have at your command, and better tools will be found as you go along." Napoleon Hill

Do all you can do on this day.

Make a start, tackle a challenge, ponder an idea, research your topic.

Whatever you do just begin.

There never is a better time than right now because now is all you have.

So the answer to the question is yes, the time is right and it's right now.

All you have to decide is what can be begun, what can be imagined or what process can you start today?

What Are You Thinking About?

"Thoughts become things. If you see it in your mind, you will hold it in your hand." - Bob Proctor

If you follow the essence of the Law of Attraction then you will know it is implicitly important to be mindful about what you are thinking about, at all times.

Simply put: like attracts like.

So, if you are thinking "I'm having a bad day" then it will stay that way.

If you flip it and think that maybe earlier wasn't quite as pleasant as you would of liked but from hereon in today is going to be much better. Then, in essence it should flow better.

One important note to add, you must feel it and believe it. If we half heartedly say 'yeah right' secretly in our mind it will cancel out your positive thoughts or words. So it isn't always easy, which is why Universal Principles receive criticism and cynicism from many.

The people who are successful are so because like anything in life the effort you put in is what you can expect to receive back.

So, it might be bad right now but it is going to get much brighter soon, feel it and believe and it will be.

And remember anything that comes up which is not quite agreeable to you, is most likely from how your beliefs are currently wired. Of course there will be riddles along our paths that test us, perplex us, bewilder and beguile us and leave us fathomless at times. But this is all part of the delightful, cosmic weaving of the wondrous world.

As you think bigger, better, brighter and bolder, then your experiences will come along matching those thoughts at some time in the not to distant future.

Flow Around Obstacles.

It's very easy to try your hardest and push and pull against the forces of nature. Do something that is hard because you feel you have to, because it's the only way (it seems).

But really you don't have to do anything. Actually you have a choice.

Rarely are we forced to do something totally against our will. We might out of love, obligation or a sense of having no choice.

If you stop and apply some Zen to your thinking you will almost instantly, or maybe after a little time, be revealed an alternative approach, a different perspective. Because usually there is one.

Our current thinking brought us to this point and our revised, expanded and deepened thoughts can take us in another direction or maybe just to sit it out for now.

Either way, the Universe didn't intend us to have such a hard time of it. Sometimes we choose it because we just can't see an alternative or indeed wait for one.

When that's the case. Just stop.

The Tao always moves around what is pointless to go through, as the natural flow will reveal itself when it's good and ready.

"Flow around obstacles don't confront them". - Lao Tzu

Keep The Faith.

Believe in yourself because no-one else will if you don't.

Believe in yourself because you are all that you have.

Believe in yourself because this life is yours to live.

Believe in yourself because you can make a difference.

Believe in yourself because that's where all majestic dreams begin.

Believe in yourself more and more as the years go by.

Believe in yourself your time has arrived.

Believe. Believe. Believe.

> "It's lack of faith that makes people afraid of meeting challenges, and I believed in myself." Muhammed Ali

Mistakes Are The Business.

This may sound kind of funny but can you imagine if you were perfect?

You looked perfect, you thought perfectly, you did everything perfectly, you were just one big fat dollop of Universal perfection, you just couldn't get any better.

Well, guess what? You are.

We are all made from the Universe and our Universe is perfect in every way, including all of the flaws, faults and imperfections.

So every mistake you make is fantastic.

Every day you think I don't look so good - you do.

Every time you think "what was I thinking or doing back then" - you did just great with what you had, knew or could do at the time in that particular mindset.

Our perfection comes in two halves - the yin and the yang, the good and the bad, the up and the down, the perfect and imperfect.

By default every single two halves makes a perfect whole and that whole is you.

Now you know you are perfect in every way. Remember that each day you make a mistake, it's a triumph because someday soon the other half of that 'mistake' will turn up and hand you a 'correction', a triumph in fact.

And note that we human beings actually love the mistakes because sometime soon when we hit a home run we can have a great big party and celebrate the good times.

> **"Freedom is not worth having if it does not include the freedom to make mistakes." Mohandas (Mahatma) Gandhi**

Do You Ask Questions?

It might sound trivial but have you noticed that those that are humble, willing to be eternal students, that eternally learn, grow and develop are usually the people asking the questions.

They are the ones trying to understand even if they don't agree. The people engaging with others, striking out bravely in their lives, despite the fear they might feel or have.

And equally have you noticed those people that don't want to know, don't want to listen, don't want to change seem stuck in a muddy field going nowhere fast seeing the same vista day in day out?

They are the ones that think staying the same is easier, is more desirable to learning and growing, like that's hard work. Okay, it might be taxing at times but we are an evolving species that is what we do, we are built this way.

So make a choice, be stuck in the mud or questioning and evolving? If needs be just keep away from the muddy ones or are stuck as they might be, they might try and latch on to you and drag you down; quick make a run for it.

> "Learn from yesterday, live for today, hope for tomorrow. The important thing is not to stop questioning." - Albert Einstein

Doing.

"Whilst doing one learns." - Dutch Proverb

Reading, listening, watching - all great.

Imitating, shadowing, demonstrating, acting, being and doing - *The* best.

A Year Planner?

If you have one take out your year planner.

Look at it.

If you are looking at the current years, see what's happened and what's to come.

If you are looking at next years, see all of those blank spaces.

Everyone is given the same one.

Each of us has 365 spaces on there.

People all over the world can sit looking at the same formatted piece of paper or an on-screen version.

The gulf comes when you are deciding what is going to happen on your planner.

That is, some people won't particularly plan much. Others may plan every single day out.

Some might have vague hopes, yet others get serious with their plans and ambitions.

So although everyone might be presented with the same bit of paper. The way we treat, react and act towards it can be completely and absolutely different.

It all comes down to your mind, your values, your beliefs and your thoughts.

That might sound ridiculously simplistic but that will depend upon your own experiences.

Whilst it may be debateable what is inside or outside of your personal control. The fact is the vast majority of your life is within it and more succinctly is precisely down to what is going around your mind right now.

So make a difference to your current and forthcoming year planners right now.

Tell it what you will be doing, where you will be going and what you will achieve in the next 12 months.

Be assertive, get creative, forget about what you have or haven't got, or whether anything is 'feasible' or not.

Stick the planner up where you can see it. Use it, write on it, stick stickers on it, colour it in, do whatever you have to do to jazz it up and get yourself motivated in to taking some kind of action.

Just think of all those untapped possibilities out there, there's another 365 little steps coming right along this way soon.

What story is your year planner going to tell?

Genius.

> "If children grew up according to early indications, we should have nothing but geniuses." - Johann Wolfgang von Goethe

Actually, you are a genius but maybe some how because of some one or some day you may sometimes feel you aren't.

The thing to remember is to take your lead from when you were a child, nothing was impossible, unimaginable or unreachable.

In the grown up world, things get a big bogged down at times, we become laden with baggage, we sometimes just forget, or perhaps just don't aspire anymore.

There is a way to link back to your inner childhood genius and that is to let go, be free and just allow yourself to be whoever you are here to be. And just follow that path for as long as it takes and of course not ever giving up.

That might sound a bit too easy. But it's a choice you can make between everything being as easy as it possibly can be or as hard as it is able to be.

Sometimes, everything being hard gets to be just too much.

So you could chuck in out that particular towel.

And you could pick up something more light and easy and free. Its your choice anyhow.

You are such a genius you know?

Individuality.

You are born with it, it lives with you daily, it moves on from this Earth with you when you do.

We might feel it is not 'tolerated' by mainstream culture, education and society. But like anything that is subjective.

Your individuality, is your signature, your character, your kinesthetic business card if you will.

Don't ever forget it, stop using it, caring for it and being a part of it.

And always be proud of your unique individuality.

> "All greatness of character is dependent on individuality. The man who has no other existence than that which he partakes in common with all around him, will never have any other than an existence of mediocrity." - James F. Cooper

A Suitable Path?

Remember your soul's purpose is happiness, your sole pursuit in life is to do what makes you happy.

The right path for you will always show itself if you allow it.

Be present in the moment and do what you can with it today.

Remind yourself everyday to be the happiest you can be with whatever your circumstance.

Greatness stems from gratitude.

So finding the right path is both critical and essential to maintaining, transcending and finding unlimited happiness in the everyday.

> "Everyone has a spirit that can be refined, a body that can be trained in some manner, a suitable path to follow. You are here to realize your inner divinity and manifest your innate enlightenment." - Morihei Ueshiba

Gesture.

A gesture of kindness, of compassion or sympathy.

Extended to another, is always returned in one form or another.

You cannot help but feel good when you have lent a hand.

And always when you need help, it will be there, when you ask or seek it.

Humans may be peculiar things at times. But you can always depend, rely and lean on some one; family, friend or a group.

Gestures no matter, how big or how small are always welcomed (by most), appreciated by someone and at the very least you have contributed to the great big gesture pot of the world.

And of course, you will receive one back, maybe just when you need it the most.

Is There Anything Else Out There?

Sometimes as human beings we can feel alone, under whelmed or overwhelmed, distracted, confused and unsure. We can go gung-ho in one direction and then quickly run out of steam, or we can spend months thinking about something and then lack the inspiration or know how of where to start.

What is this all about? Essentially we all ebb and flow like the sea does, we can go up and down in everything that we might be, do or have. Remember though that you are always receiving signs, suggestions, prompts or nudges from your inner self and the Universe.

Learn to take time to really listen to how you are intuitively feeling, what you are thinking and about whether what you are doing or thinking about is really something that you actually want to do.

Additionally; fear, procrastination or some good old self discipline might be stopping you from starting, progressing or really flying.

Accept it. You are a living breathing person so you are entitled to waver from time to time. But remember you are on your own personal journey through life. And there is always something else out there, whether that be a new direction, a new idea, help and support or whatever it might be.

Keep a look out and keep checking in with yourself. You are doing a fantastic job, so tell yourself so.

Give yourself a pat on the back, take your self out for a treat. You deserve it.

Another bonus is the kinder you are to yourself, the more amazing you will become; everyone loves to be loved and appreciated, it gives us that unlimited power that we all have within.

Roller Coaster.

They say life is a roller coaster, filled with ups and downs.

You may have experienced that for yourself and know of others that have too.

The funny thing about roller coasters is some people love them and actually travel around the world to experience the best there is whilst some people avoid them altogether throughout their whole lives.

Interestingly we use the analogy flippantly because it's an old one. But in the present tense we can decide which roller coaster we are going to ride and whether we are going to enjoy it or not!

Sometimes the fast straight parts of the track are invigorating and for sure many people scream at giant dips and falls and loop-the-loops and many people are laughing their heads off by the end of the ride.

Surely then as you view your year, month or life, as a series of roller coasters, the ups and the downs, the vivaciously happy and the moments of sadness, the sometimes scary and sometimes submerged but at times laughing so hard it makes you cry.

Maybe we should actually be smug and keep smiling because you know what, we survived the ride, we are still smiling and what a lot of stories we have to tell from all those experiences.

It's all good.

Purpose, Vision & Goals.

"Your purpose explains what you are doing with your life. Your vision explains how you are living your purpose. Your goals enable you to realize your vision." - Bob Proctor

Take each of them seriously and separately. That is ponder and go within to find the true answers that belong to you and only you. No-one can tell you what is right for you but it is something that can be inspired within you, that can be awoken, that can lead from one place to another.

As there are no set right and wrong answers, it's ultimately down to you but your current results your current stance in life will give you an accurate summary of what has gone so far. Is it to your liking? Does it feel right? Are you on track or course? Have some things been forgotten? Are you pushing aside any true goals?

Over time we all evolve so sometimes it's no surprise that these things might change shape somewhat. However, other times you find you knew all along, it's been there with you for a long time but maybe you lacked the clarity, the courage or the knowledge you thought you needed.

From when time began until when our time ends, humans only need their intuition to guide them, the rest is down to resource, asking, finding, journeying.

Anything is possible and many have conquered the 'impossible'. So can you.

Is Your Character Yours?

Can you think off the top of your head what percentage of you is really you?

What parts of you have you decided upon and what have 'others' decided for you?

What beliefs, culture, values, ideas, judgements and so on are yours by choice or by default of your growing up and evolution around other people?

There comes a time when we need to review our own character, values and beliefs and renounce that which was pushed upon us, or force fed through school or any other organisation or social places, that no longer or ever did serve us. To ensure we are filled with that which we are totally congruent with.

When you go through your own set of values and beliefs you can very quickly determine those that are you to the core and those which are not.

Simply because your intuitive response is most likely one of feeling or knowing, it can be kinesthetic, or one of rich pictures, sounds or tastes.

Essentially our inner self holds dear those things that truly mean anything to us and everything else that might be found rattling around without much effort or conviction.

It is hard to fight a battle in which you are not really present. So why bother?

Your character is yours and no-one else's so choose carefully, wisely and mindfully what you put in to it as it's inner content is mirrored in your actions and behaviours and if you don't like those much, you know where to look don't you?

So take a trip down memory lane and find what still stirs you, fires you up and gets you moving and those things that make you feel lethargic and none to fussed. Tip those out and you'll find renewed vigor in what really counts to you.

Your character should be the sum total of all that you feel is essential to the way you live your life and can contain any single element that you wish. Each is as unique as a finger print and takes a lifetime to mature and blossom.

On that basis select your ingredients and tend to them well, as these are a long term investment in to the physical and spiritual being of your everlasting soul.

Give Up?

"Give up and you will succeed.' - Lao Tzu

Have you noticed that when you are really trying to do something or get a project finished on time, or find an object, or maybe make a particular item and so on and you just feel like you are fighting and getting nowhere fast?

Have you ever thought better of it and just stopped as though you have given up because it's just not worth the effort?

And then have you found the thing you were looking for, or you get a message that the item isn't needed after all, or the printer just miraculously starts printing again on it's own or maybe a better idea comes to mind, to hand or from an e-mail or a conversation?

That's the art of recognising what is a challenge or an obstacle that you should continue with and what is the opposite of the Tao leading you against the direction you are meant to be headed.

Sometimes we just need to stop and check that. Usually your inner guidance will 'speak' to you and let you know to just give it up, let it go and go with the flow not against it.

Usually it won't work out well anyway, so save your energy and motivation for those pesky elements of goals that actually will require it.

The right way always shows itself, we just have to be willing to see it.

Super Strong Diversity.

Have you seen a pick 'n' mix shop or counter?

Hundreds of different flavoured, coloured and sized sweets and treats. Children can't wait to choose their favourites. Maybe adults sneak a few too.

When you view the world like a giant sweet shop and see the variety we humans come in and our diversities and differences. We are surely glad that we are so lucky to be such a rich, beautiful mix of eclectic people.

Imagine one day waking up and the whole world was say, green. Yes, everything and everyone was just one shade of green.

Can you imagine that for a minute and how terribly dull, boring and drab that would be to your clever eyes?

We are super strong because of our diversity, we are unique yet the same, we are worldwide yet a community, essentially we all want love, happiness and fulfilment.

Yet how we choose to pursue our lives and how we live them is up to us.

We are able to go and grab our bag of pick 'n' mix and put in it whatever takes our fancy. And yes that means you can change your mind.

Gosh aren't we lucky, fabulous and super special too?

Do You Have A Pet?

Pets, animals and wild life all share something wonderful.

They have evolved and been around for thousands and thousands of years.

It is probably no mighty coincidence that when you are sat stroking your cat or out walking your dog or tending to your pets that a sense of calmness and balance is restored within you.

Their presence is ageless and transcends in to our busy frenetic modern world.

Be still, be calm, eat, sleep and be happy.

Be grateful for what you've got and exert moments of emotion as and when they are needed, nothing more.

Smile and take a deep breath.

It's all good.

Begin.

Today is the day to begin. Start now, there will never be another day like today. Think of one thing (big or small) which you could in some way start right away. Maybe research, booking an appointment, purchasing software, enlisting a coach, opening a new savings account, giving some money to your favourite charity, writing that business plan.

Every single nudge is one little step closer to your aspirations, dreams and goals. Importantly, when you make that tiny bit of progress you will be able to know you have done something because you will always feel encouraged, inspired or motivated after you've taken any step of action.

> "It's the little things you do that can make a big difference. What are you attempting to accomplish? What little thing can you do today that will make you more effective? You are probably only one step away from greatness." Bob Proctor

Time For Tea? (or Coffee).

"If a man has no tea in him, he is incapable of understanding truth and beauty." - Japanese proverb

When working, sometimes people feel as though they cannot stop. There is so much to do, places to be, and people to please.

Sometimes though, you are the 'to do' item, you are the destination and you are the one you need to please and nurture.

Every day find yourself at least ten minutes or so and sit with your favourite beverage and do nothing in particular. This could be listening to music or just have silence or contemplation time.

Tea ceremonies have been around for thousands of years because people knew that 'chilling out' was as important as 'getting a move on'.

The yin yang of life will always bestow it's reign on generating the right amount of each.

Truthfully you know when you are tired and you want to rest, conversely when you are rested you want to take dynamic action.

You already know this but sometimes you deny yourself because of 'stuff' and being 'busy'.

Please don't forget about yourself, you are a very important person in the Universe, after all it wouldn't be the same with out you would it?

So how about taking five or ten minutes now?

There's no reason not to make the time.

Decisions, Decisions?

It has been observed that 'richer' people make fast decisions and stick to them and 'poorer' people take longer to make the decision in the first place but then frequently change their minds. This comparison has been made in financial terms only; as we know people feel different levels of abundance in other areas of their life too.

The point is if you have financial backing even though you know that everything isn't going to work out in every minute detail, as everything in life never does, you still have a secure, grounded feeling. However, when you are on a tight budget and you are 'worrying' whether you have made the right decision or not, hence the often frequent change of heart. So essentially, a rockier financial position leaks in to your self esteem, self worth or self confidence and can hamper other decisions. And in some cases can dramatically affect whether a person will take a 'risk', or attempt to conquer a challenge and so on for 'fear' of affecting the status quo in their life.

So speaking of heart, we must remember that the more we make decisions based on our gut instincts, intuitions and that 'just have a feeling about x, y or z', then the better. Are all of those decisions going to work out perfectly? Probably not but when you make a decision based on your intuition alone as opposed to your bank account or what other people think and so on, then this will work out the right decision for you for one reason or another. Such as, meeting someone new, a different perspective, a new idea, an old idea growing into a better or bigger idea and other variations.

In addition the more you actually do make decisions and keep moving forward the more likely it is you will increase your income at some point and the more easier it will be to make fast decisions and stick to them. In any event it will increase your self confidence and that always has it's own rewards.

Remember every result is just feedback, review it and move on. And every single person on this planet is making, receiving and thinking about a decision at some point today.

Some will work, some won't work out but so what, you are alive in the moment and doing the best you can. As hard as it maybe, try to remain true to your inner guidance and go where ever it leans towards as this is far more likely to be better for you than making decisions based on circumstances alone, as they do not factor in things the Universe hasn't even let on to you yet.

So, today - make all of your decisions intuitive and stick with them. It will work out right in the end for you, the Tao knows what's best for you, so just keep on walking your true path.

Let's Pretend.

We know that children pretend a lot when you watch them play, they pretend to be this and that. And they'll use objects as something else whilst role playing and generally using their imagination at every available opportunity.

Adults don't like to pretend much if they can help it. It is as it is and that's that. However, when you are goal setting, when you are planning on your future in any area at all. What you are doing in essence is 'pretending', you are seeing yourself being, doing or having whatever it may be.

If we could rekindle our childhood inhibitions of entering our imaginary world on a daily basis, then things will move on faster for us. By remembering that energy is everything and that we become what we think about the most. Then every single idea that we pretend is coming to fruition will kick start every level of our ability to make that happen. For instance if we talk about something, we draw a picture or use imagery, if we feel what it will feel like and so on.

When our combined senses are evoked regardless of whether it is currently true or real we begin to develop that mindset, those behaviours and we can literally transform our dreams in to our realities.

That's not to say, there might be issues, challenges and set backs along the way, that's likely inevitable but what is proven is that if we truly 'believe' that which we 'dream', then we can surely 'achieve'.

So pretend away, make a list, go through it daily and make it feel real, until one day it is.

Give Away Riches.

"To be able to give away riches is mandatory if you wish to possess them. This is the only way that you will be truly rich." Muhammed Ali

Learn to live with grace and servitude, be happy to give and live with abundance.

You can fill your cup as high as you like, so long as you keep emptying it so that others can share it's rewards too.

Did You Get What You Wanted?

Ever wanted something?

Did you receive it or not?

How long did it take?

Have you noticed that it depended on the intensity of the desire for the item in question, the goal itself?

If thoughts become things then be careful of the wording.

So if you want a 'dream holiday', you get to 'want a dream holiday'.

If you set a goal saying I am going on my dream holiday in August for example, your brain will then kick in to action to help facilitate that goal.

So for example your action steps might include looking at brochures, flights and hotels or anything associated with the trip. You would then have a set of dates to work to and a cost.

Then you might set aside a certain amount of money per month or if you have it already book the date, location and flights.

The essential ingredient is how you word something and what your intentions are.

Lots of people 'want' lots of things but do they really desire them? Is it something they will work consistently through issues, challenges and hiccups to get? For a lot of people the answer is no, they won't.

So when deciding on what you 'want' make it a succinct list of definite goals to be included.

Cast off any might(s) or should(s) as they are just not cutting it.

Three steadfast, absolute certainty goals of what you are aiming to be, do or have are collectively worth far more than a long list of wishy washy drivel.

> "The imagination is a dream factory of which realities are a by-product." - Richard Wilkins

Priority.

What do you consider a priority?

What is more important than something else?

When do you think you should work on the items on your long term goal list?

How do you stop being distracted?

How much time is acceptable generally surfing the internet?

Did you really do all you could do yesterday relating to the 'be, do, have' decisions you have in your mind?

Do you really believe you can do it?

Are you truthfully right now trying your very best?

Is it other people that 'appear' perfect (but you know really that they're not) that put you off even trying?

Is self sabotage a better acquaintance to you than your self esteem and confidence?

What single thing could you do right now that would make a difference?

Is there anything you can action today towards tomorrows dreams?

If you can set up a daily reminder or calendar notice indicating - 'Dream Work', 'The Future', 'Do I Want X Enough Time', 'Today's Action Step' or whatever fits you best.

And just take a single step each and every day, it doesn't matter how small, as they all add up to a bigger stride and sometime soon you'll be within running distance of that goal.

> "A journey of a thousand miles begins with a single step." Lao Tzu

On Time Or Late?

Which one are you in the habit of?

Which one do you prefer to see in action?

Which one do you prefer to offer the recipient of your next appointment?

Our choice to exercise our self discipline and be punctual (or early) reflects our respect of our time and of others'.

It announces your character as someone who is reliable and sound.

It eludes that you are in control, organised and in charge of your destiny.

Your time, my time, our time - is precious, so why would we waste it on being late?

If time is something we cannot stop, control, erase, rewind or pause, it is then one of our most precious resources and should maybe be treated like gold?

Measuring time, evaluating time, speeding up and slowing down our actions in time, using it wisely and precisely are all available for us to use at our discretion. It just requires some discipline, contemplation and maybe a list or two!

Next time you are late or some one else is, if never you, think about the reflection upon that person and the rest of the day.

Whilst a few minutes here and there might sound a bit unnecessary to get worked up about. What if we add them all up over a week, a month, a year or gulp, a lifetime. Do you think that time could be put to better use?

Today.

What's so special about today? Well let's think about it for a minute shall we?

Well it is unique, there won't be another one along like it.

Today's date, won't happen again.

Where ever you are, whatever age you are that won't ever be the same again either.

What happens today in the world won't be repeated the same way, with the same people in the same location, ever.

Today, then is really extra special. We should cherish it and not take it for granted, not moan at it because of our problems, challenges or issues.

Let's celebrate today, and give it all we've got and then be grateful we had it in the first place.

What could you do today to remember it by? Well you could write in a journal, make an entry in your diary or do something that you will remember. Or just enjoy it with someone you love, watch a film, go out in nature, dance and sing, play games with your children, go out on the town, sit down with a cup of tea, read a good book, whatever it is you love to do.

Above all just enjoy yourself.

Keep on Walking.

"It is better to walk than curse the road." - Wolof, Senegal Proverb

It's okay to take a rest, it's good to take in the view but what we must not do, is stop.

Only when you stop do you allow in anything that could, would, or does stand in your way. Those old acquaintances, fears, doubts, negativity and so on.

So what we must always do is keep on walking....

When Will Wisdom Come?

"Wisdom comes only when you stop looking for it and start living the life the Creator intended for you." - Hopi, Native American Proverb

Your present knowledge, life experience, thoughts and actions have led you thus far. Be it fabulously good, interesting,or maybe not so great, either way it is always challenging, amazing and vital.

Your inner wisdom comes from the guidance of your higher purpose. Once you are tuned in to the correct station it is virtually impossible to not live that which you were born to. Unless of course, you choose to change the channel, that is up to you.

Many of us tuned in to it as children, for they know nothing else as they are born of purity, but as we grew, we dithered and dallied and tweaked the dial here and there and then sometimes it seems, we find ourselves on an altogether other frequency. We wonder how we got there and if there is any hope?

Later on we might purposefully choose to re-find this perfect station of ours or we might feel we cannot quite remember where or what it was.

But worry not, deep inside, like a magnet, you can always be re-tuned in to your own inner wisdom, it is there ready and waiting for you. All you have to do is ask, be patient and follow your own path, the Tao always presents itself.

Calm.

"Meditation is the soul's perspective glass" - Owen Felltham

Take the time to make the effort, to calm your mind and be present. You have so much happening on a day to day basis that at times it seems futile to even try.

But know that the reverse is true. If you can successfully manage your mind, your time, your purpose around the seeming chaos of the world, you will find a new level upon which you can strive and organise and make some progress, no matter how small or slow it seems.

And remember this, you are not alone, lots of people around you are trying to figure this out too. The only difference is those who having staying power and don't quit know that their goals are worth the effort and those that either haven't set any goals or whose goals don't inspire them to make the effort, so they ultimately give up.

You won't give up will you? Because you know in your heart that giving up on your dreams and goals is giving up on yourself and who on earth would want to do that?

So remember from time to time to stop, to just be calm and peaceful. The soulful you will thank you for it.

Are We There Yet?

When is it the end? The end of a goal, of a chapter or an experience.

Truthfully the only real end is the end of our time here on Earth. Until then, there is no end.

Each of us must therefore, keep going, ever striding, we may have some stops and breaks along the way but we mustn't let our spirit stop seeking, our curiosity stop asking questions and our minds thinking we know all the answers, even when we know we don't really.

There will always be a new perspective, a fresh vista and an alternative vantage point. Our in-exhaustive quest as both individuals and a species is within is and makes our progress truly staggering. Yet our minds haven't even really begun their work yet considering we are not at our capacity; we are still only getting warmed up.

> **"When you reach the top, keep climbing."** - Zen Proverb

The Art Of Balance.

> "I believe that being successful means having a balance of success stories across the many areas of your life. You can't truly be considered successful in your business life if your home life is in shambles." - Zig Ziglar

Everyday, be mindful that your entire life's happiness is dependant on how good you get at being in balance and harmony with yourself and all around you.

It's easy to spot when you are out of balance: ill health anything from headaches to dis-ease, bad moods , from tempers to tantrums, feeling stressed, over whelmed or even under whelmed. Not being very kind or caring to others or to yourself. Too many bills, too little time, family demands or not having any. These imbalances can be all from many areas of your life and can come in all sorts of forms.

The binding of it all, is you. So delve in to your intuition; how do you really feel about the various aspects of your life? Some might be great or okay, where as others might need dire attention.

With balance you can work on one thing at a time and concentrate on putting anything that 'feels' wrong right. We all need fine tuning though, so it's wise to oversee every aspect of your life and maybe diarise a monthly check in to check up on yourself and see how you are doing.

> "Just as your car runs more smoothly and requires less energy to go faster and farther when the wheels are in perfect alignment, you perform better when your thoughts, feelings, emotions, goals, and values are in balance." - Brian Tracy

Imagine.

Imagination is everything. It is the preview of life's coming attractions." – Albert Einstein

Cultivating the imagination should be compulsory.

An every day time out for a little imagination or maybe even a lot.

Using your mind in this way is like an aerobic workout.

You need to use those brain cells, push and pull them, incite them in to doing something new, different or awkward.

We cannot continue to improve if we stay the same.

Instead, we can make those incremental ascending steps with some intense working out of the mind.

You could for example have an 'Imagination Journal' and each day write in absolutely anything that comes to mind.

In order to stimulate your mind you need to be calm, relaxed and free from all persistent distractions. To be able to move in to the zone where your mind just wanders and has a play around in the vast playground that is your subconscious.

Anything can happen in there so do not limit yourself to what you think you can or can't do just because your logical mind says so or even your egotistical self for that matter.

There are no boundaries inside the mind it is free to wander the wonders of the Universe and back again.

So go take it for a walk, no lead required

Music can help get in to the imagination zone, as does silence and walking in nature too.

Who knows what you can imagine out of the ether.

Let's get that 'Imagination Journal' open and see what we can do.

Enough Courage?

How much is enough?

Can we ever have enough or too much?

How about too little?

The thing about courage is, it's free and you can help yourself as and when you need it.

So go pick up a big bucket and fill yourself up with as much as you like. As with so much in life, no-one else will do it for you, they might 'assist' you, motivate or inspire you but at the end of the day you've got to make that journey and go get it.

> "He who is not courageous enough to take risks will accomplish nothing in life." - Muhammad Ali

Whole Health.

Have you noticed how a lot of people are lopsided? Maybe at times so are you?

Lopsided is when someone sacrifices one aspect of the whole self for another.

So let's say you eat amazingly well, in fact better than most and you put others to shame at how good you are. But do you make the same effort for your self improvement and your mental and spiritual health? Maybe, maybe not.

So whole health is when you are mindful and act as much as you can in your own best interest of your complete self. Your whole health is like getting four cylinders running rather than one out, one flagging, one half hearted and one rearing to go wondering what's up with the other miserable lot.

They are not miserable really, they just need your tlc (tender loving care). You and only you can give yourself whole health t.l.c.

    "The greatest wealth is health." - Virgil

Who Cares?

Have you ever thought about who really cares what you think, do or be in your life more than you do?

I doubt anyone cares more than you do about what you do with your life.

If you are your most important fan, critic, supporter and overseer of you, then you may as well do your very best, achieve your optimum success and live the life of your dreams.

For no-one else is going to come along and care more than you, be able to understand you like you do and do anything about what it is deep inside you.

Yes other people do care about and love you too but guess what, they have themselves to runaround after too.

So remember to be kind to yourself, listen to what you have to say, how you feel, what you are seeing and thinking right now.

Take time out to be your own best friend, as you are more qualified for the job than anyone else around here.

> "You are the only problem you will ever have and you are the only solution. Change is inevitable, personal growth is always a personal decision." - Bob Proctor

Possibility.

Is there a limited number of possibilities in your life or do you think they are unlimited?

Whatever you answered, you were right.

Clever isn't it?

> "You already possess everything necessary to become great." - Crow, Native American Proverb

Stick With Your Ideas.

Remember to stick with your own ideas. If they are right in this moment and time, then you will find a way. If they are wrong then that's for you to find out and learn whatever you needed to learn.

Do not take to heart other people's lack of interest, the naysayers and their friends. They are either jealous of your idea or you, incapable of thinking of one of their own or maybe they don't want to see you succeed for whatever reason that might be. But remember that's their problem and not yours.

You will always gravitate towards the positive people because they will always say 'go for it', regardless of whether they think it's a good idea or not as they know that is for you to find out.

Every person is on both yours and their journey too and most want to spur you along, just like they want to be spurred along too.

Take the happy bunch along for the trip and leave the others behind.

> "Every revolutionary idea seems to evoke three stages of reaction. They may be summed up by the phrases: 1- It's completely impossible. 2- It's possible, but it's not worth doing. 3- I said it was a good idea all along." - Arthur C. Clarke

Our Earth.

What else could you be doing to help the earth whilst you help yourself?

Small things, big things - any kinds of thing will count.

Whether we recycle more, buy more consciously, teach our children great habits, help those worse off than us, give to our community - every person has a choice and an opportunity to contribute in a positive way.

Maybe once a month take a little time to review what you have done this month maybe journal it and then see if you can improve, refine, share and take notes from others and let other people know what you are doing - it might inspire them too.

By every one learning, growing, participating and getting great at doing these things we can make both small and big differences.

Your difference counts, you count.

> "Treat the earth well: it was not given to you by your parents, it was loaned to you by your children. We do not inherit the Earth from our Ancestors, we borrow it from our Children." - Native American Proverb (Tribe Unknown)

Comfortable?

Are you comfortable? Is it all feeling easy?

Or do you on a regular basis s-t-r-e-t-c-h yourself on any levels of the mind, body or spirit?

Comfortable is okay when taking a rest, a nap or when convalescing but for everything else you need to be exposed to periods of feeling uncomfortable, uneasy, not sure and a little scared.

Because you cannot ever truly learn anything 'new' without going through a bit of discomfort. We know on the other side of trying, learning, developing and growing there is that 'comforting' feeling of triumph, success and happiness that we did it.

> **"Man's mind, once stretched by a new idea, never regains its original dimensions."** - Oliver Wendell Holmes, Jr

Partial.

Dictionary adjective:

being such in part only; not total or general; incomplete:

Aim to ensure your goals, dreams or day to day lists are not full of things you feel only partially motivated to do.

As physical, mental and spiritual beings we are far more likely to take massive action on those things we feel driven to do as opposed to obligated, forced, or coerced in to.

Okay, so someone has to do the dishes, feed the cat, entertain the children and so on but these are life's ongoing routines and rituals, that you have to take in your stride.

What we are talking about here is the list you would like to look back on, say when you are 100 years old and as you look down the long list of ticks, you will feel you did the best you could, you made the most of it all, you grabbed all of those wonderful opportunities and you went out and created some others along the way.

And not a person sitting and saying 'if only'...

So a partial yes or no is not good enough, it won't cut it, it won't light the fire and burn bright in the sky.

Remember to say yes to those things you really truly mean yes to and be big and bold and say no to all of the rest of it.

Growth.

Observation about the Universe:

Have you noticed that the more 'it' appears to push you, the deeper you dig and whether you like it or not you get through, you survive and sometimes radiantly glow?

And the results well, let's just say you've grown, you keep growing and you keep amazing everyone around you. There really isn't anything you can't do when, as they say you put your mind to it.

But you know what that really means is that you are in tune with yourself, your surroundings and your Universe and when that happens.

Watch out - your unstoppable.

But you know that already right?

The Point Is?

The point it seems, is to find one. If you have a purpose, a point, a goal, a destination or other in mind, then you may proceed.

If however, you don't have a point and you find yourself aimless, well that could mean you are destined to fall on to the someone else's path. And really, can you rely on or expect any other person to know you better than you know yourself? Can you really expect them to deliver what you need to be your best self, when they are so busy figuring out their own path? No, I didn't think so either.

So what's the moral of the story? Make sure you check in with yourself, every day if needs be, check that inner compass, check you are on your track, going your way. That doesn't mean solitude, loneliness or unkindness, or even selfishness. All it simply means is that you have a point to your very being and the task is to figure it out, then hand those insights back over to the Universe which will pass you clues, mentors, opportunities, both good and not-so-good times as you are guided along.

One thing though, don't expect these 'things' to always be obvious as they might not be and of course, some might be wrapped in positively 'terrible' times but underneath the wrapper, there is a gift, an experience, a new friend or new found purpose lurking inside every one of them.

So keep your eyes peeled, keep your purpose in mind and take it as it comes. Are you ready? Off we go then….

> "Great minds have purposes, others have wishes." - Washington Irving

Dreamers.

Have you ever noticed a poignant split in us humans between those that 'talk' about this and that and never actually do anything.

Especially those that like to criticise others particularly of that which they have no experience in. And those that rush about 'doing' all sorts of things but lack direction, planning and purpose.

We then disappointingly have the minority who have dreams, formulated in to goals, detailed in to plans, with bite size action chunks and to boot ensure they are surrounded by other like minded people, have mentors and motivators and keep on learning, growing and taking inspired action regardless of whether they feel like it or not.

Something amazing happens doesn't it? If you know of an example of each type of person, think about how happy they are, what they radiate whether they are positive or negative, do they quit or never give up and any other characteristics they might exude.

It may then come to the surface that no miracle has actually happened, that a combined, consistent and persistent approach wins the day, every day, without fail or exception.

And anyone ever having walked this Earth has only achieved and manifested their dreams by trying, understanding, learning and applying. And at times, over and over again.

So today, let us be that minority and join the club that is going places.

> "The world needs dreamers and the world needs doers. But above all, the world needs dreamers who do." - Sarah Ban Breathnach

Admiration.

They could be the admiration of everyone.

It maybe that admiration was the primary motivation.

Possibly admiration was how they got there in the first place.

But none of that is important to you.

At the end of the day the only persons admiration you want, need or need to bother seeking is your own.

You may have noticed so far in your life, you cannot please everyone, someone somewhere disagrees with you, you cannot get along with everyone and would you want to anyway?

Seek your own approval, reside with and by your own values, give some of your affection to yourself.

Happiness by definition can only be attained by your own values because you set them.

Having some admiration for yourself, what you have been through, how you got to here, from where you came and from where you might be headed.

Worry not about other people for they are busy sorting their out own 'stuff'.

Your personal admiration begins with you, once you have it you can give it.

But you cannot give something you don't have inside you already.

> "It is not because the touch of genius has roused genius to production, but because the admiration of genius has made talent ambitious, that the harvest is still so abundant." - Margaret Fuller

Circumstances.

Have you ever said 'if circumstances were different I would .....' or if someone asks you to do something or go somewhere you might reply, 'well if circumstances allowed I would' and so on..

The problem with the word 'circumstance(s)' is that it is in the past and if you notice we are giving 'it' the power and not ourselves.

Let's dig a little deeper.

You right now are a by product of your previous circumstances.

You are at this moment in time experiencing a certain circumstance or set of circumstances.

However, your future which is in the next minute, week, month or year is your future circumstances.

So really you don't need to lean on the excuse of circumstance(s) you need to see them like a piece of clay, something you can shape in to something more pleasing to you, or something you might want to tweak and in some cases you might want to start over with a fresh piece.

You are 'allowed' to do that, the Universe will accommodate whatever change in future circumstances you want as it is your intent that counts.

But remember if you don't ask for help, you won't get it. Think about what you want, write it down, talk about it and go out there and action it.

Those circumstances will appear sometime in the future if you are ultra persistent and patient enough.

But whatever you do, don't forget that today, we are talking about past tense.

And you know already "the past doesn't equal the future" (Anthony Robbins), so why drag it along with you?

Acres Of Diamonds

You may be familiar with the story or not but the crux of the story and subsequent speech made all the way back in 1890; is about a man who feeling unfulfilled and not finding riches, sold up his property to go off in search of diamonds, following a journey and a long quest for riches that he didn't actually ever find in his life time.

Ironically, right back on his former land that someone else had bought and worked, ironically found diamonds, indeed a whole mine of them, hidden within that very land. Riches were indeed abundant right under his very nose.

So, essentially the message is to search within.

Look around you.

Take closer notice of what you do have than that which you don't - or indeed think you don't.

Be prepared to dig deeper in to the resources within yourself that already exist.

Do not be put off by what your mind or others may say is possible.

You are your own 'acre of diamonds' there is more untapped wealth within you, that you might not even be aware of.

You are a perfectly created gem, a jewel, a gift from the Universe.

Some people may appear a little rougher around the edges, some people may be all about the shiny appearance.

But inherently within us all, is the capacity, the depth, an unbound resource, unlimited aptitude, power and potential.

Philosophically speaking we all have access to the same amount of acreage of diamonds but the finding, observing, taking and tending of it, is purely one of personal choice, change and optimistic ongoing pursuit.

Either way you have a front row seat, whether you sleep through, take notes or leap in to action is all up to you.

Carefree.

Are you carefree?

Is anyone carefree?

Can we even be carefree?

Carefree by dictionary definition - is to be without worry or anxiety.

So yes there's hope. You too can be carefree.

We all know 'worrying achieves nothing' so that takes care of that. It's a waste of our time, energy and focus. We simply have to remove worry and focus on something constructive, practical, tangible or inspirational; something that will get us moving away from worry and not clinging to it.

Anxiety, well that's almost worse. Is by dictionary definition living in fear of, non-doing because of what might happen, distress and uneasiness of the mind, danger, apprehension. Makes you feel anxious just reading that, doesn't it?

It might be easier for some and harder for others. But for true balance and harmony of your whole self, then you simply must practice living and breathing with a carefree attitude. Your health of mind, body and spirit is dependant on it.

It doesn't mean you will never ever have obstacles, issues, baggage, annoying people, bills or the likes but it does mean you have total faith in yourself and the Universe.

You can deal with whatever it is. You will find the way, the answer or the solution. And you simply will be fine and dandy.

Maybe a little affirmation might be in order:-

"I am carefree: I have everything I will ever need to be happy, healthy and wise".

"I am carefree because I have the Universe in my corner".

"I am carefree and far too busy living and being happy to worry, I'll leave that to the worriers".

Use those or make your own up, then put them on the fridge, on your computer or wherever you like as a reminder that you can be 'carefree'.

Concentrate.

Have you noticed the more you concentrate on what it is that you a, want to be doing b, should be doing (over say, procrastinating) and c, what would make your life better in some way then this happens:- the better you feel, the happier you become and the more congruent you are with your own thoughts, feelings, values and so on.

Funny that isn't it? On the flip side if we become fixated on the media or on the trivia of who's doing what, where and with whom we can make ridiculous comparisons on some occasions to our own lives or we might even become despondent or wonder what the point is in anything.

So really the one thing you can do for yourself today, tomorrow and the day after that is to concentrate on you. You are the one you are counting on, you are the one that can make the difference and you are the only one that can decide what's best for you and where you are headed.

Perhaps take some time and ponder on what small thing or big thing you can do today to concentrate your efforts, thoughts and beliefs upon to move you one step closer to your dreams, aspirations and goals.

Small consistent amounts of concentration that turn in to massive action came make giant amounts of difference.

A Combined Harmony.

"Happiness is when what you think, what you say, and what you do are in harmony." - Mohandas (Mahatma) Gandhi

Essentially things are just about as difficult or as easy as you decide they are. Regardless of whether you understand or not, or how much effort or action it requires.

Simply, if we focus on thinking thoughts that are conducive to our goals, speak only words that are in alignment with those thoughts and walk forward in our actions in a combined harmony.

It eventually becomes like those first steps of an infant, up and down, wobble and fall and then in no time at all those steps become stronger and longer, faster and easier.

It is no coincidence that behind everything you are here today, sits your mind and thoughts as they single handedly got you here. Thoughts can virtually with no persuasion at all take you some place else if you'd rather.

So what do you think? What's it to be?

Have You Found It Yet?

Are you still searching or have you found it yet?

What is it you are searching for? Do you have any idea? Or are you waiting for something to appear or maybe you've lost hope of it ever turning up?

Tricky isn't it, the balancing act?

Let's simplify things.

Only you really know you. So the answer is in there somewhere.

You are the one that really knows truly and deeply what it is you want your life to look like.

You are the perfect architect, dreamer, creator, director and administrator of your deepest desires.

What matters is what you think, not them (the others) what do they know?

Keep in touch with the real you, write it down, draw it, visualize it do what ever it is you need to do.

Go and sit somewhere alone and just 'be' for an hour or so.

It's amazing when you let go, how easily things will flow around your mind.

It's highly likely you will have obstacles, life is going to dish up some pretty tasty problems, dilemma's and just plain old tough times on occasion.

But you know the thing with life and the Universe is, if you yield to yourself, help yourself and move forward in a positive manner, give of yourself to others. Then it's like, metaphysically speaking, brownie points are growing somewhere and when you ask for a 'top up' or a 'withdrawal' one will arrive when you need it.

The trick is to be open and flexible. So let's replace searching for being open and flexible. Keep moving forward on your life's dreams and slowly but surely it will start to happen, just have patience and resolute belief.

It's never too late, you are never too old, too thin or too fat, too rich or too poor, or lacking in this and that and the other.

As the saying goes; 'Carpe Diem' - seize the day.

Is today good for you?

Let's begin .....

What To Do?

Decisions, choices, actions, consequences, mindless errors, lucky punts, going with the flow, nothing to lose, easy come easy go, treading water, thinking about it, not sure, maybe another time....

It's been observed that successful people make decisions quickly and recall them slowly and not so successful people make decisions really slowly and change their minds frequently.

Whilst we could debate on the word 'successful' and what it means to you. What is interesting from that piece of information is this.

If you are confident and happy and have good levels of self esteem and generally are feeling good about life, there is no doubt you will be operating from a closer position to your true self and more congruent with your intuition, gut instincts and so on.

If on the other hand you are feeling pretty low, unhappy, unsure, stuck, confused and similar then you will be operating from a position further away from your true self.

On that basis we can see quickly the best place to be to make swifter decisions and fewer mind changes can't we. Obvious, yes? Easy? It could be.

Belligerent isn't usually associated with a positive word but if you are just that you can be in connection with your true self and you will make better decisions, feel better and the cycle will strengthen and the habit, well it becomes habitual.

Everything is as we decide to see it. That then is our choice and another decision.

So if we are quick and stick to it, and say 'bring it on' regardless of what it might bring. At least we know that we did in fact, make this decision to the best of our ability and although it might not go perfectly, we are getting better at it every day and that will keep the positive momentum building.

Empty & Full.

"First on the battlefield

Waits for the enemy

Fresh.

Last of the battlefield

Charges in to the fray

Exhausted." - From The Art of War by Sun- Tzu

When you are on time (or early), prepared, thoughtful, considered and organised you give yourself the upper hand.

You are calm, in control and able to deal with whatever circumstance or sets of events are about to occur. You can ponder, decide, communicate and concur with others.

If you are late, unprepared, mindless, ignorant, disorganised, neglectful then you give yourself no hand at all.

You are at the whim of what you have arrived in to, you are having to instantly react and give a knee jerk response.

Which would you rather be?

Which works best do you think?

Take a look at others around you and see which category they fit in to. It can be an enjoyable observation which you will soon be an expert in, instantly deciding who is from the fresh team and who has arrived dishevelled and exhausted.

It might be a good idea to let on to your secret of being so punctual and organised and well prepared.

It's secret is using a dairy, a clock and some planning.

Do you think it might catch on?

Pass The Buck?

Have you ever wanted to or actually have passed the buck?

Think about it, how many of us actually want to have the buck stopping at our door every time?

Maybe not always? Ultimately, we have two choices. Take full responsibility and accountability and deal with it. Or spend most of our lives slipping and sliding, blaming others, saying woe is me and other such non productive thoughts.

Next time, don't even think about passing the buck. Just grab the thing and say 'yes that's me' I'll take that one on the chin. And get it done with.

We could easily have made a mistake, a wrong judgement, an unsound choice, decision, investment, we might have the wrong end of the stick, not have all the facts and the likes.

But generally the quicker we grab that buck, the quicker it passes and the faster we can get on with something else, much better. Your mind can get on with far more important thinking tasks on the horizon as well as enjoying the moment in today.

And of course, the stronger, more confident and more self assured you become to boot. Shall we bring it on then?

Poverty & Want

"There are no better masters than poverty and wants."
- Dutch Proverb

The balance is ensuring we leave no one behind in poverty, without food, water or shelter and that we discipline ourselves that having 'things' is fine to a degree but not to the point that our time is a slave to our wants for then we have lost our pure sense of freedom.

Some might say you can't have it all but they are usually the same people that can't figure out how to.

You can have all you want providing what you want is in balance with the Universe, if it's not then you won't have it for long. But if you just crave material items, then you'll have all the want and longing you can get, the Universe will surely deliver that.

It provides all you need and more. So just be careful for what you wish for or more precisely the words you choose, the context and the detail.

We are here to aspire, improve, ascend and become fuller and free and help others to become so too.

Are You Lucky?

Have you noticed the kinds of the things people say are 'lucky'?

Some circumstances appear very fortunate like near miss accidents for example.

However, most events aren't really down to luck are they?

They are a result of actions, or in-actions and their subsequent consequences. Or cause and effect.

Admittedly some might be out of your direct control such as a company closing down and it's employees suddenly being out of work. Or someone driving recklessly and creating an accident.

However, the vast majority of life's 'luck' falls under one banner and that is having the knowledge, insight, planning, preparation, organisation, due diligence, mentors and so on being stacked in your favour and not against it.

Luck sometimes has the acronym 'Labouring Under Correct Knowledge'.

When you look at it like that. You can suddenly understand that even the slightest bit of misinformation, lack of knowledge or understanding, incorrect information even can drastically alter the steps you are making, are about to make or have already made.

With this knowledge in mind, take more time to stop and think. Really think about what it is you are currently doing, about to embark on or are considering doing.

Try to make extra special effort in preparing, researching, finding others that have walked the path before you.

There is absolutely no luck or coincidence that once you crack the code of correct knowledge that you need to succeed in absolutely anything. That you will find yourself having a far greater level of success than you would have done without it.

Essentially, most people do not bother with this essential step, they plunder, blindly around in the dark, dimly following a very rough course of what it is they are doing. Of course, worse still there are those that have no plans or goals whatsoever and you know where that leads them.

So take a long look at 'luck' and decide will you be blessed with your very own home grown luck; for you will take great care garnering and gathering that correct knowledge so when you do 'labour' for your fruits, people will say, "you are so lucky - everything just works out for you".

And you can smile and know that much more than luck, today you are both wise and the Way - one with the Universe.

Moving On To Higher Ground.

Think of each level, each stage or section of any process as one where you may rest and re-think, enjoy and benefit from. But one that at some point will move you forward to the next aspect of the journey, challenge or lesson you are currently amidst, advancing you to higher ground.

But one thing we must remember is not to limit ourselves, not to constrict our future based on our past, not to dwell on too many details of why we can't do something but rather on the fact that there are boundless, unlimited, options, opportunities, chances, stages or parts and each of them has infinite potential wrapped up inside them.

> "If you always put a limit on everything you do, physical or anything else. It will spread into your work and into your life. There are no limits. There are only plateaus, and you must not stay there, you must go beyond them."
> - Bruce Lee

Stepping Stones.

Stepping stones can be big and small,
they can be slim or they can be fat.
You can take a rest on one today,
And survey the others far away.

Stepping stones are all for you although
they seem to hide from time to time.
Sometimes they can light the distant way
But know they are always here to stay.

Remember your steps are perfect and light,
they show you the way and bask in the night.
Stepping stones are holding your hand as
Mother nature graces the land.

Remember you must never quit or lose sight,
that another will appear when the time is right.
A stepping stone is a great friend for life
Helping you through both glee and strife

So never dismay as all will be well my friend,
Stepping stones are here until the very upmost end.

Afraid Of The Dark?

We all know that we create our own fears don't we?

But still when you were a child and the light would go off, the imagination would flick on, noises, shadows, imaginary monsters and whatever else we could conjure up would instantly appear. We might be frightened and we would maybe shout for someone to come or go and switch the light on just to make sure.

But if and when you make a firm decision that actually there is nothing there, that it's your imagination and you are in control, then those things simply disappear? But if you let your guard down, if you forget you are in control, in creeps your imagination and you are back to the start again. This is a good picture of our minds parse.

You are in control, you decide what pictures are going on, what audio is on and at what volume and you get to decide if you rule your emotions or if they rule you.

Sometimes as to be expected we temporary lapse, forget, get lazy or distracted. No worries, this can easily be rectified. Just be mindful that you are creating those negative connotations that you have the power within to flip them and turn them in to a positive at will.

Yes, it isn't always easy and alas we may stumble and fall. But just like the child coming to terms that darkness isn't anything to be scared of, just like them we can quickly get over it.

> "Fear is that little darkroom where negatives are developed." - Michael Pritchard

Your Greatest Enemy.

"The greatest enemy of knowledge is not ignorance, it is the illusion of knowledge." - Stephen Hawking

It is most likely that for your ongoing personal success, you need to remain humble and be the eternal student.

A teacher of one subject is a novice at another.

We are all clueless about something, regardless of how much we think we might know. For everyone there is always something new to learn, fresh perspectives and areas we have absolutely no understanding in.

It is far more sensible and intelligent it seems to remain in awe, forever learning, open to new thoughts and possibilities. To ponder a new premise or have to read something twice because you just didn't 'get it' the first time.

A child like reverence of our world will keep us curious, optimistic and knowing that anything is possible well in to our 90's or even 100's.

So today, let's surrender to the fact, we don't know it all and though we might never will, what we can count on is having one incredible journey, many memories and experiences whilst trying to figure it out.

Filling our knowledge buckets up as full as we can get them along with embracing, experiencing and expressing life will help keep us healthy, wealthy and wise and a lovely interesting person to know also.

Colourful.

Sometimes it might seem that life's not so good.

Other times it's a vibrant cabaret of joy.

But at the end of the day, we live a very colourful life and grateful for it we should be.

Without the array, diversity and spectrum to see, we wouldn't be so lucky to live, breathe, see and feel such colourful lives.

Thanks for that Universe.

We appreciate it, really we do.

Woolgathering Is It A Good Thing?

Idle daydreaming is something that is positively discouraged in most schools.

Being away with the fairies is definitely not acceptable when you're an adult and supposed to be working.

Yet, every philosopher, inventor, creator, artist, writer and ideas generators are all inextricably linked by their shared love, persistence and competence in enjoying their woolgathering.

To day dream, to sit and let the mind wander, meander and indulge in it's idiosyncrasy is anything but a bad thing.

It is to be wholeheartedly recommended, developed, explored and mastered.

So today be a non-conformist or every day if you like?

Spend as much time woolgathering as you wish for you never know what yield it has for you and where you'll be headed next.

Happy Woolgathering Day.

> "It is absolutely essential that before we begin to think, before we so much as begin to set our thinking in motion, we experience the condition of wonder." - Rudolf Steiner

Definitive List.

Okay, today's the day.

Out with the paper and pen.

On with the thinking cap.

Off in to wonderland it is.

Drift for as many minutes as you can.

Now from your intuition set down those absolute must have items from your inner be, do and have list.

Not maybe or possibly?

Just nailed on yes's.

It doesn't matter if there are 3, 5 or 10 (or more or less) things on there.

1.

2.

3.

4.

5.

6.

7.

8.

9.

10.

Write them out daily. Chew on them over dinner. Dream about them.

Now as time goes by keep checking that they get your pulse racing i.e. that you do still actually and completely want to accomplish these goals.

Cross off any that no longer apply.

Alter and adjust whatever you need to.

Keep them fresh and bang up to date.

Do not take your eye of the ball - well the list in this case.

Tick off the action steps you have taken.

Celebrate every step along the way.

Keep on going as you will soon be there, regardless of whether that is 1 year or 10, yes you will soon arrive.

You can do it. The Universe shares your definitive list and is lighting your way.

Chaos Or Order?

"If you think you can have order without chaos, you understand nothing about the laws of the Universe." - Chuang Tzu

Some days nothing seems to go right, perhaps things just feel pressured or maybe you just can't seem to make any noticeable progress.

Just relax and remember that everything happens in perfect order, for the Universal Laws happen instinctively and regardless of what we 'believe' in.

So a good day follows a bad day and an even greater day may follow after a huge monumental 'problem, issue or challenge'.

That is the Way. Yin follows yang, and yang circles yin.

You are on your way and you will get there. In fact you may have arrived already or even slipped past your exit. Either way it will correct itself in the end.

Be Very Weary Of The Word 'Lack'.

Lack is often used to describe that which we don't have enough of.

Lack of time, lack of energy, lack of money, lack of friends, lack of opportunity, lack of self esteem, lack of skills, lack of holidays, lack of wisdom, lack of family…

Lack, lack, lack.

We should however, be very weary of the word lack and use it seldom if at all.

The more lack we discuss, the more lack we will attract.

The more lack that lands, the more lack that never ends.

To break the cycle once and for all.

Banish the word, never to repeat it again.

Change it to content, that you are happy with who you are today and what you have and that you would like to improve, extend, increase, provide more of and feel more abundance instead.

> "Be content with what you have; rejoice in the way things are. When you realize there is nothing lacking, the whole world belongs to you." - Lao Tzu

Recycle.

Do you recycle?

Some people wouldn't dream of not and some people can't seem to dream of a reason why to begin.

When we recycle, we accomplish so much more than we might even know.

We are of course contributing to the action and intention of stopping the littering, destroying and hurting of our planet. So singularly the right reason to do so regularly.

But we are also teaching our children a lifelong habit.

We are informing our minds, creating a habit of being conscious of how we buy, use and dispose of anything at all. And also allowing ourselves to be more creative and use our resources in a better more organic way.

Collectively as we work together for the greater good of our Earth and us, the dwellers upon it.

We have a chance to view our purchases multiple times, from the shop, to our home, to the cupboard, to the sorting out of the recycling, so we can decide whether there were good choices or not maybe? And make any alterations next time.

Our minds when presented with a challenge, a change or an alternative decision, get to broaden, strengthen and develop every time.

There are so many things we are learning from this one decision, from your home perspective, your community, country and your planet.

We have no idea where this will lead, what will be invented, developed or created.

But we do know that everything we do that's positive for the better, makes a difference and an impact so you know you can say you are changing the world, in even the smallest things that you do.

Without you, it wouldn't be the same.

Keep up the amazing work.

Rain.

"No person has the right to rain on your dreams." - Martin Luther King, Jr.

No-one.

Not ever.

Not once.

Not twice.

So let your sun shine unharmed, radiant and expressively free.

A True Friend.

"Hold a true friend with both hands." - Kanuri, Nigerian Proverb

True friends may be hard to come by, the ones you can depend on, you can confide in, the ones that truly support you and want you to be the best you can be. So to, in return you can give them all that and more.

Treasure them and remember them from time to time. Everyone is busy but everyone needs a friend sometime. And remember to let them know who they are as they might not know just how important they are.

Beautiful.

…..admirable, alluring, angelic, appealing, beauteous, bewitching, charming, classy, comely, cute, dazzling, delicate, delightful, divine, elegant, enticing, excellent, exquisite, fair, fascinating, fine, good-looking, gorgeous, graceful, grand, handsome, ideal, lovely, magnificent, marvelous, nice, pleasing, pretty, pulchritudinous, radiant, ravishing, refined, resplendent, shapely, sightly, splendid, statuesque, stunning, sublime, superb, symmetrical, taking, well-formed, wonderful

These are examples of words from a thesaurus derived from the word 'beautiful'.

Have a look around you today and the rest of the week, month and year, at nature, at our world, at your family, at anything else you like and see if you can see, spot, or be overwhelmed with as many of the above adjectives as you can.

P.S. pulchritudinous - what a word.

Are You A Big Shot Or A Little One?

What was your answer?

Hopefully you answered both.

You are 'big' at some things because you've been doing them for a long time and 'little' at another because you might be fairly new to it.

Either way, to get to be big, you just keep on trying....

And whilst you are doing that you get to keep adding more 'little' things to your repertoire too.

> "Big shots are only little shots who keep shooting" - Christopher Morley

Peace To All.

"It is no longer good enough to cry peace, we must act peace, live peace and live in peace." Shenandoah, Native American Proverb

Reflect all that which you radiate, value, hold dear and true.

If we aren't completely congruent, happy or honest with what that maybe, then there is always time to change and act.

Our good intentions, values and beliefs we must share and never stop.

After all you make all the difference, so you must begin with yourself.

A small improvement to one person at a time sends a ripple right around the world when shared.

Are You Secretly Happy?

At the most deepest core of all of us is the natural and instinctive pre-disposition towards our own happiness.

We might have learned along the way that other people's ideas and things that we yearn for one day or another is not necessarily the way for our true pure happiness.

If we bless ourselves daily and allow our natural state of happiness to shine through we most often find we can tolerate life's bumps, dips and dents that little bit better.

And the best bit we don't have to wait for anything or anyone we just decide to be happy right now. Are you in?

> "No matter what you are doing, keep the undercurrent of happiness.
>
> Learn to be secretly happy within your heart in spite of all circumstances." - Paramahansa Yogananda

Could You Cry?

"Don't be afraid to cry. It will free your mind of sorrowful thoughts." - Hopi, Native American Proverb

It is vitally important for our mental, physical and spiritual health to let it go.

Your troubles, worries, grievances, resentment, anger, disappointments and hurts.

Glean what you can from them, use them in a positive way. But pack them off and rip them up in to tiny little pieces of paper that can be burnt right out of your mind.

Dysfunctional behaviours don't serve us - we know that but still they keep on when we allow them to.

Be strong and allow your soul to shed its tears so it can move on and journey long on to better times.

Miracle.

"Impossible situations can become possible miracles." - Robert H. Schuller

What seems to be an unconquerable circumstance or experience clears the way to a new found clarity, reason, purpose or opportunity.

Possible, plausible, doable, thinkable, achievable are found always in the mind first, in reality afterwards.

Grace.

...is a way for us to help control our emotions rather than them controlling us.

If we can find some values and characteristics within that we believe in most passionately and then allow them the room to shape us. Rather than our dysfunctional ones such as anger, jealousy, bitterness and so on controlling us and leading us to somewhere we ought not to be.

Over time what ever we exude will greet us on our return and we will at once be free of the hold our emotions once had upon us.

> **"The ideal man bears the accidents of life with dignity and grace, making the best of circumstances." - Aristotle**

Touch The Earth.

Take time today (or soon) to walk in nature, breath it in, see it's treasures and feel it's wonder.

We never fail to feel something when we are at one from where we came. Is that any surprise? Maybe we just forget or are too busy but nonetheless it's important to your soul and that soul is all of your past, present and future, so that makes it's wishes extremely important doesn't it?

> **"To touch the earth is to have harmony with nature."** - **Oglala Sioux, Native American Proverb**

Are You Your Own Master?

"He who controls others may be powerful, but he who has mastered himself is mightier still" Lao Tzu

We have all seen it and most likely done it. We lose ourselves somewhere and our emotions take charge. We are at the mercy of our fears, our anger, our manipulative ways, our emotional blackmail, our rages, our breakdowns, jealousies or insecurities, fears and an array of others we might be akin to.

What we might not have noticed is the synchronicity between the degree to which we can maintain a calm and orderly house in our mind and the degree we can expect our dreams to be fulfilled.

Generally speaking the Universe will pass on to each of us a set of opportunities, circumstances, rewards or mediocrities that fits with the way we think of ourselves, behave and conduct ourselves.

Help yourself and remember that being mindful of this is one way to allow an easy flow in and around you and your world.

There will be challenges up head that's almost certain, so why make it any harder? At the end of the day, the final word is yours, so what's it going to be?

Back To The Start?

When you were young, you already knew.

When you see children at play or they say something seemingly profound. They instinctively know.

Our connection to Source was and is very strong. But as we grow, as we study, as we are influenced by those around us, by technology and trend we can drift off our inner course.

But if you take the effort to go back and remember you'll notice you carried with you the answers all along. Obvious it may or may not be but the pointers, the hints and hazy paths were there all the same.

Generally that which you felt was the right path, was. Today, that may have led you down other paths but that would also be correct, as that stemmed from your original Source path. And remember that which you feel to be right now or tomorrow, probably is.

Sometimes we might get confused, digress or stray but none the less when we are ready, our way, our path, our inner clarity of source will be ready and waiting.

> "If you would know yourself, take yourself as the starting point and go back to its source; your beginning will disclose your end." Proverb from the Ancient Egyptian Temples

True to Yourself.

"Live your own life, not the life that others say you should." - Lieh Tzu

Today, just remember to consider yourself in all areas of your life, to be true to yourself and to be good to yourself.

They say you can't give what you don't have. So if you don't make yourself happy, then you are unable to contribute your positive energy to anyone else.

Do what you think is best for your own life and happiness.

You might be forced to listen to others but you do not need to heed their words or let them in emotionally.

You know what is best for you.

So live your life the way you want to live it.

Begins In.

"Wisdom begins in wonder." - Socrates

Traits of the wise in training could be:-

Curious

Coachable

Enthusiastic

Note takers

Goal setters

Organised

Creative or

Entrepreneurial

Listeners

Meditators

Contemplators

Energetic or

Outgoing

Thinkers

Doers

Never quitting

Or ever giving up

Taking failure as feedback

Experience collectors

Travellers of all kinds

Strong values

Morally strong

High integrity

Their word is their bond

Thoughtful not thoughtless

Considerate

Kind

Compassionate

Philanthropists

Happy to help

These are just a few you could surely add more but the essence is you are far wiser than you think and have more wisdom coming to you than you could ever use.

Be mindful that wisdom needs you as much as you need it. Without each other your both stuck.

Maybe consider the traits of 'stuck' people?

Ignorant, unhelpful, belligerent, angry, bitter…..

Humorous?

Quick, list 5 things, people, programmes, images, jokes, sayings or experiences that make you laugh a little, smile a lot or split your sides hysterically.

1.

2.

3.

4.

5.

Of course you can go on for as many as like.

But keep your 'humour list' somewhere where you can see it or find it. So when you are feeling non too pleased, despondent or just having one of those days, you can look at it and laugh, or even a small smile will suffice.

And you will feel so much better or happier.

Aren't you already?

Yes You Can.

Worry not about what you think you can and can't do. Focus on what it is you really want to do and just move forward from the beginning point.

There is nothing more important in your life than being clear, succinct, passionate and inspired to be, do or have whatever it is you see, feel and want of yourself, now and in the future.

The rest is academic, you will learn, you will grow, fresh opportunities will arise, enticing paths will open and some will close and then change direction, over and over.

Your No.1 priority is to be crystal clear on your purpose, on your goals, values and expectations.

Do not focus or worry or sweat the small stuff. It's just not important in terms of getting going, of course details will count later on.

Think big picture. Dream those grandiose ideas. Feel excited for today and tomorrow and every eventuality, idea or inclination.

For they will become whatever you believe them to be.

> "Men often become what they believe themselves to be. If I believe I cannot do something, it makes me incapable of doing it. But when I believe I can, then I acquire the ability to do it even if I didn't have it in the beginning." - Mohandas (Mahatma) Gandhi

Window Of Opportunity.

Sometimes it seems we are forever waiting and other times it seems they just miraculously appear.

Whatever guise they come in a window of opportunity will be your intuition telling you it's right, it's okay, it's time to take action, go or stay, wait or pounce.

Are they always correct? Maybe not it might always seem at first glance.

But you can guarantee it is better to grab with both hands every window you feel is right because a result, feedback or conclusion is going to turn out positive or negative. If it's positive then you'll be glad you took it and if not so good then at least you will have learned something.

Better that than someone in their twilight years sitting on a mound of closed windows, wishing things could have been different - when actually they could of.

> "Opportunities are like sunrises -- if you wait too long, you miss them." - William Arthur Ward

This Is The End?

Is it?

When do we know?

How do you know that this is it?

The end?

The end of what exactly?

You have so many endings in your life just as you have so many new beginnings.

It's all about what we focus on.

We could just sit here staring at the current end we are facing, feel down, despondent, desperate even.

Or we could set off a party popper and blow one of those children's blowouts that make a big noise!

And maybe throw in a merry dance in you feel like it.

So never forget it. Let's celebrate.

> "Every end is a new beginning" - Tai Gong Diao

Abundance.

Abundance is a funny thing and could be quite easily a catch 22. For example you might want to give but you might barely be supporting your own family, so you could feel guilty about not giving and resentful about not having enough to give. Sometimes even, you might feel you be giving or doing more than you are already.

If anything like that ever happens in your mindset, here's something you can do immediately to change it in to a positive:

Only good will come from your positive thoughts, feelings and actions.

So remember what you do have for example your health, your family, friends and anything else you are blessed to have - a nice garden, a car, holidays, days out or whatever is true for you.

Do this on a daily basis no matter how you feel or what 'mood' you are in, choose to tune in to the positive frequency.

Once you feel your gratitude for what is good in your life you can then see more clearly the abundance that is already right here with you today.

Abundance is all over our Earth and we can help others by being there, having manners and offering help. Even giving the smallest amount of change might not feel a big deal but think about the person receiving it?

It can often feel bigger to them that someone cares and

that when you give when you are not financially wealthy it counts because it shows you are caring, kind and compassionate. And of course if you are wealthy then think how you can give and in what ways your money can be the foundation for something more substantial. Or maybe a long term commitment or project for you to be involved in.

There are many ways to feel abundance and to share it. Sometimes we get so caught up in the every day it is easy to forget, to maybe moan and not really do all that we can do.

You are abundance as you are part of the Universe, you can give it and take it too. But remember it all starts with how we can help someone else first as this connects us to our Source then we feel significance in that we are contributing which then empowers us to do more and be more and then later on of course this can translate to having more too.

> **"The Universe operates through dynamic exchange… giving and receiving are different aspects of the flow of energy in the Universe and in our willingness to give that which we seek, we keep the abundance of the Universe circulating in our lives." - Deepak Chopra**

News.

Do you like watching the news?

Do you know why?

How much of your time does it take up?

Is it worth it?

No-one can tell you what to or not to watch, or whether to bother watching at all.

But you can from time to time check to see what you are doing with that spare time of yours and wonder if it could be better spent.

News can be good or it can be bad, similarly inspirational or tragic. It may or may not affect you personally. It might be fine for five minutes at a time.

But think of your time being like a piggy bank and you can save it up for something spectacular, monumental and outstanding or let it trickle away, flittering and feckless on something you can't even remember.

Some people say no to any kind of news apart from good news. Some people watch every type of news available.

Maybe you could just check out what and how you are viewing your news and similar items and decide what those piggy bank time pennies are going on this week and see if you want to tweak, save or spend any?

Not Just Yet.

"Before receiving

There must be giving". - Lao Tzu

Keeping an eye on your giving cup allows the natural yin yang balance of the Universe to flow.

The Universal order will allow your cups to flow in and flow out. Ebbing and flowing just like the tide.

We all have two cups - one for giving and one for receiving all as one.

This is one set of books that is in everyone's best interests to keep balanced.

So don't forget to take a weekly peek in to how yours are looking and balance them if needs be.

Is It Fear Of Failure Or Feedback?

What is it that we fear the most as human beings? Is it our fear of 'failing' something, looking stupid or proving the naysayers right?

Or do we fear what feedback may result from whatever it is we are doing?

What do you think? The combination of all of those might be true in most human nature.

So let's flip it. Forget failure, scrap the word, erase it from your mind.

Most big achievers or people with high self esteem and the likes are the same. There is no failure only feedback which basically is an outcome of one sort or another. Whether it may be fantastic or dreadful, it's only a result that constitutes feedback.

At the end of the day, you are going to be making some mistakes in this lifetime. The choice or the knack is to go quickly from any feedback you receive which is not to your liking and diving straight in to the next step, albeit with some insights, considerations and alternatives. So that means just getting on with it and not dwelling, moping around or licking your wounds for too long.

Every single super successful person, whether that be financial, career, fulfilled dreams…whatever.

All have one thing in common. Tons of feedback.

So let's spin it the other way and remember, 'Every day in every way you are getting better and better'.

As this is the case, accept feedback as being like golden carrots moving you ever closer to the feedback you are striving to receive, it could be just around that corner at any moment.

Today, be grateful for all the feedback for all of those outcomes for they are truly splendid indeed.

You know what not to do; you know what works and what doesn't. More importantly you know what you are capable of so far and what you are prepared or not prepared to do.

So let's stack them up and pile them high. We're aiming for the heavens and we need all these 'outcomes' big and small as rungs to our ladder.

Hope you've got a head for heights because that's where you're headed.

> "Before success in any man's life he is sure to meet with much temporary defeat and, perhaps, some failure. When defeat overtakes a man, the easiest and most logical thing to do is to quit. That is exactly what the majority of men do."- Napoleon Hill

Can You See Past The Clutter?

Every now and again do you find yourself wondering how things seem to pile up? Swamped with mail, e-mail, to do lists, filing, the 'I'll get round to it pile' and much more?

Even if you are highly skilled and trained in time management it really is a never ending asteroid belt of things flying at you from all angles isn't it?

What can you do right now to get the following results?

Less stress.

Calm environment.

Feel on top of things as opposed to feeling over whelmed.

Be able to work at your pace and not 'theirs'.

Breathe.

Take some time off for yourself.

Indeed, you may have other things on your list and some may resonate with you more than others. But here is a researched observation that could help you now, today.

First of all, we all have the same amount of time available, therefore do not impose upon yourself unrealistic, fantasy type deadlines and work loads that clearly you cannot complete in the unreasonable time frame that you have either self imposed or been given.

What you can do though is this:

Get really clear on your lists of what actually needs doing and when by.

Sort in to order of importance and priority.

Add in any dates and times you are working too.

Take 5 minutes and really assess your list.

Okay, so now we need to see what things really have to be done like now, today, immediately!

Get rid of everything else on the list you can possibly defer, delete or delegate.

Now in your diary, organiser, online calendar and so on, mark in that one job or maybe several smaller ones and a couple of really simple quick ones.

Okay, this should now make you feel more focused and less stressed by the other 'stuff' as we have now moved that out of the way.

First things first, get the most important high priority job done immediately, that is no procrastination of taking care of the little jobs to get some ticks on your list.

Forget everything else and work until this is either completed, passed to some one else, or awaiting further input, resources, research or whatever else.

Once you have done that then move patiently, diligently and calmly through the remaining small tasks.

At this point now stop. You have done what had to be done. You do not need to peek at anything else on the list. Give yourself a well deserved time out.

The more balanced your approach, the more self disciplined you get with this, the better you will perform and thus your successes will increase.

And also add on there, either daily, weekly or monthly or whatever suits you best to go through your desk, get rid of clutter, get rid of junk that you will not ever get around to. File things that you need to keep.

Ensure you schedule all the 'you' time appointments in your diary too. That way you can't forget, ignore or side step yourself.

Successful time organiser's all share the same secret. They are fiercely competent about their to do lists, they compile them the day or night before so their brain has absorbed the tasks and therefore when you get up you hardly need to look at your list as eventually you get in to the habit of going straight to the most important task first above all else. Plus they schedule in anything that enhances their personal, emotional, spiritual or financial development.

Simply put if you are operating at your maximum level and you have systems in place that serve you, the more on top of it you are, the better you feel, your results will improve and there's time to enjoy your family and social pursuits.

Like everything it can take time to become a 'habit' but it is something you can do today and enjoy the benefits of this evening. Try it and become a ruthless clutter clearer.

Repetition Is The Mother Of All Skill.

"It's the repetition of affirmations that leads to belief. And once that belief becomes a deep conviction, things begin to happen." - Muhammed Ali

Have you noticed that the more you try, the more you train, the more you do, the better you get?

Have you noticed the more you put something off, create fears and excuses the bigger they seem to be?

Have you noticed that if you really, truthfully want to do something you will?

If you really don't want to do something then you will find a way not to.

Don't waste your precious time then on things you have no passion for, move them aside for those that you do. Repetition is the mother of all skill for a reason - it works, so let's not change a fabulous system, let's perfect it and see what we can really do?

Honesty.

No matter what always be honest with yourself. That may sound rather obvious but really your honesty matters a great deal to you. If you are true to yourself, honest with yourself and remain in touch with your intuition then you can't go far wrong following your life purpose and living your own life.

What's important isn't so much what other people say to you or about you, or what the media is reporting on at this moment, it's all about your integrity and honesty. It is so easy to become lost in the whirlwind of life and lose touch with yourself.

So if you have your honesty to yourself as your best policy then you know you can check in and appraise what's really going on. Happy, sad, good or bad, it makes no difference we are all playing our parts in the giant yin yang song of life.

So, honestly, how's it going with you right now?

Wu Wei.

The art of non-doing or in-action - wu wei offers a note worthy inclusion in to our day.

By keeping our intuitive lines open and acting spontaneously in a way that is in line with our own inner guidance, and also that of the Tao. We are able to creatively come from a stance that is the opposite to one of forced action or intent. It enables us to find a more natural harmonious and congruent outcome.

The difference then in our outcome is one that is a natural action stemming from our choosing of being in a state of wu wei versus that which is an unnatural action which can come from our uncomfortable, harassed or overwhelmed state when we are doing, or acting in a state that emotionally doesn't feel right or natural to us.

Above all. Remind yourself that wu wei is natural action. This comes from within us but can be produced at will because our natural harmony is in alignment with the Universe and not against it.

At the end of the day you know when something feels right and when something doesn't, when decisions flow versus when they stutter. You naturally had wu wei down all along, it is just worthwhile being mindful of it from time to time to nudge yourself in the right direction. And remember when its best to simply do nothing at all. The way will always open up and become clear.

Are You Feeling Grateful Today?

"Gratitude is an attitude that hooks us up to our source of supply. And the more grateful you are, the closer you become to your maker, to the architect of the Universe, to the spiritual core of your being. It's a phenomenal lesson." Bob Proctor

Let's understand one more thing with gratitude. Here's a question for you:-

When you are feeling negative, speaking negatively and cursing or moaning and generally being negative do you :-

A. Have a totally fantastic, productive day of joy.

B. Stub your toe, spill coffee, get mad at everything and everyone, getting more annoyed and fed up as the day progresses.

C. Realise you have slipped unwittingly in to negative land and decide to laugh, to smile, to pay a compliment, write in a gratitude journal or similar?

It's all about choice, self discipline and self knowledge. You know it but do you do it?

Remember this then, the more hours we waste in negative land the further away we get from our dreams and goals.

And the more hours we spend, gravitate towards and work on visiting positive land then the closer we get to our goals and generally enjoying life.

Sorted. Let's get on with living in positive land.

Are You A Pessimist, Optimist Or A Realist?

> "The pessimist complains about the wind; the optimist expects it to change; the realist adjusts the sails." - William Arthur Ward

Catch yourself if you fall in to pessimism by lifting yourself on to optimism's breeze then driftingly ponder what realistically can be done in this moment.

We all might possess all three in different doses but the trick is to be mindful of which one we may be consciously or unconsciously languishing in the most. Then make changes to alter your course and be flexible when required.

This is a 'secret' success trait of the highly successful. It isn't actually that difficult is it? It is just being mindful, flexible and consistently persistent.

And you can do that already.

Your Favourite Colour?

Do you have a favourite colour?

What is it? Think of one now if you don't.

Try to put something of that colour on your desk, in your car, work top, bag or where ever you are likely to look in the day.

Something that conjures up some good, positive, emphatically great feelings.

If you can and one exists, get a pen or high lighter or similar of that colour and write or underline or highlight any task which you keep meaning to do and do not get around to.

A lot of people think colour therapy is very conducive to encouraging harmony, balance, or motivation and passion even. Alongside being an important element in Feng Shui. So if you put your favourite colour and therefore energy around something that you keep meaning to do, then essentially you'll see the colour and 'feel' better about doing what ever it is.

At the very least it might help you get it done as quickly as possible so you can continue on in your revived and uplifted mood. That can't be bad can it?

And of course, colour your positive to do list up a bit too whilst your there.

Your Repertoire.

Have you ever listed all of your skills, knowledge, experiences, techniques and wisdom?

Probably not and no we are not talking about a boring old CV - the epitome of average.

You might not yet be able to see the value, the benefit or the point, so let's delve deeper.

In life there is a habit, as you know, of people being loud or shouting when they are complaining or moaning, are disappointed or are generally not happy, outraged, disgusted, shocked and other such feelings and emotions in a variety of circumstances.

We probably realise that there are far less compliments, good job notes, thank-you's and generally 'you are fabulous', 'what a great skill or technique you have in your work' and the likes flowing around the world right now.

It's a real shame and something we can all contribute too if we put our minds to it.

But when you list your good points, your skills and life experiences you get to see a visual picture of who you are and what you can offer. You also get a crystal clear picture of any gaps, holes or areas you are ignoring, missed or forgotten.

You might for instance think actually one of your skills is a little outdated, you might want to join a course to learn something new, you might be able to teach someone else what you already know.

In fact the possibilities are endless because your repertoire is like your DNA, it is unique to you. The big difference is that with DNA we get what we are given at birth and we are to be jolly grateful for it. But your repertoire is something you can re-invent, re-invigorate and re-ignite at will.

You could take a look at it each month and see what you can add, update or maybe cross out and replace.

The choice is yours and the options are amazing.....

Second Thoughts?

How many second thoughts have you ever had?

Could you really count them?

Probably not.

Do you think there has been a person on the planet that hasn't had a second thought at one time or another?

It is doubtful isn't it?

We are clever mammals not robots. We think, we are uncertain, unsure and worry. Sometimes we just can't help ourselves.

The fastest way to get over this little hiccup is to go through worse case scenarios.

That might sound a trifle simple but if you grab a sheet of paper and note down the current issue in hand and on one side put down the best case outcome and other side worse case outcome.

First of all you are addressing the worst possible version of events. And really are they that bad? Will you stop breathing altogether if they happen? Probably not.

A lot of worse case scenarios are uncomfortable and not particularly wanted. Which is a huge world away from living somewhere in complete poverty, with no food for your dying child and family, no roof and no government help and no real options at your fingertips.

At the end of the day, we should focus on the best case scenario and make progressive daily steps whilst taking inspired action to help that become our reality. If for one reason or another we find ourselves creeping towards the worse case scenario then we accept it, it has done it's worst then, it is over. We need to dust ourselves down, stand up and move on again and again until we get back to our left side of the page and the more wanted and desired outcome.

It might be a tad annoying and disconcerting but we usually find in there a big old fat life lesson. We have learned something, we become richer for our experiences, especially the tough ones.

You will find that the more you experience of this, the better you become and the more able you are to help yourself and potentially putting a cherry on top by you helping someone else too; as you can empathise, understand and really make a difference to some one else's world.

Second thoughts are natural but what we do with them is a choice. Every single time.

Choose wisely.

> "Act as though it were impossible to fail." - Dorothea Brande

It's Time.

If you've ever watched a big Mixed Martial Arts event, then you'll have heard the compare with his loud unmistakable voice, shouting loudly for the main event

"Ladies and gentlemen it's time……." then he goes on to introducing in the red corner and so on..

What's always striking about this phrase is:

It never sounds old hat because he says it with purpose, conviction and meaning.

He introduces every fighter as a 'warrior'.

The audience really does believe it is time - right now because it truly is.

How's this important for you?

Well in the morning do you announce to yourself 'it's time'?

Time for you to be your best self.

Time for you to go out and get whatever it is you truly 'want'.

Time for you to stop making excuses about what is preventing you doing x, y & z.

Time for you to ignore other people's opinions, dreariness or non support.

Time for you to shine

Time for you to live and be all that you could ever be.

The actual crux of the matter is that now really is the only time anyone of us actually has, we really cannot predict what is around the corner but we can have a solid and firm - belief purpose inspiration and action - to get out there and do it.

It really is time - so enjoy it.

Lost In Translation.

Many things are often passed off as being 'lost in translation'. But the reality of it, is that really most of our lifetimes communication is 'lost in translation'.

The reason is that you think differently to the person you are communicating with and therefore what you are saying, writing, drawing, articulating, designing, creating and so on can only be received, interpreted and transcended in the way that they think it is being transmitted or how they choose to perceive it.

You most likely have had, like everyone else on the planet, moments of despair, of hair pulling and quite possibly anger when the other person 'just doesn't get it'. They don't understand you or what you are trying to communicate.

As hard as it maybe, we have to let it go. Do not worry about them, the others. It's not their 'fault' as they think differently to you, so why are you wasting your precious effort.

This doesn't mean we shouldn't try, of course our eternal human spirit is driven by evolving, improving, saving and inspiring.

What it means is the realisation, the acceptance that we can learn to improve our communication methods and we can aim to have our concept, idea or conversation understood but after the fact that it is out there in the Universe, then we have done our bit, hopefully our very best and it's life beyond that will be whatever it is so intended to be.

It may be difficult and sometimes painful. It could be frustrating and yet at the same time we might feel a huge weight is lifted because once you have let it go. It's gone. Floating away off in to time and space.

The best anyone can do is a journey of self education, the discovery of human emotions, temperaments and intelligence. We can learn to improve, to understand, reason and grow. But we cannot expect everyone to think the same way we do as the Universe hasn't intended this to be so. And what a dull place that would be.

We exist, unique yet conjoined together in our personal and communal Universe.

Live it and let live.

How Strong Are You Feeling Today?

Check out what your to do list is today, maybe reflect back on what it was yesterday.

See how much you did achieve or what you plan to achieve today.

You will notice some key themes.

That which you are driven, passionate and in full belief of, you will get through no matter what.

That which is weakly driven, boring, or disliked, you will drag your heels, sigh and moan and maybe procrastinate.

No coincidence of course, that which is your purpose, your passion and your bliss you are eager to tackle (even if you don't really know what you are doing or how you are going to do it) and will take precedence over the mundane or that you feel less inclined to do.

There are several ways to tackle the rest of the stuff you have to do, taken from those that do what they love most or all of the time.

Delegate every single item out to someone else that loves to: do accounts, organise & clean, do DIY, gardening, housework and other blanks you can fill in.

Now before this leads to any negative resistance, let's just review this. Some people trade jobs with others in their household for example one person cooks, another does the laundry and so on. Usually in every example of our unfavoured jobs there are some items we are more willing to do than others.

Secondly, if you can invest the fee for someone else to, for example do your accounts, cleaning, car maintenance and so and then you are free to do more of those things you love and yes, to in part pay for the person to do the things that they enjoy doing to.

As a side bar this takes us back to our bartering past, we exchanged the goods and items we made or sourced for others we wanted. The only difference today is that we 'expect' ourselves to wear all the different hats of all of those professions and yet can't understand why we can't 'do it all' and for some 'perfectly' so whilst they are at it.

Let it go, you know you can't be all things to all people. And bothering to be only means you miss out on being the true you. This is a pointless exercise.

Alternatively, do what you love for the first part of the day so that the most important 'work' is done first and have a single minded approach to go through the rest of the important or urgent items. The idea is that you are in a good mood having done the good stuff so you can face the not-so-nice stuff and just get it done.

Conversely, some people may prefer to steam through the not-so-nice list first so they are rid of it for the day and spend the rest of their time on the good stuff. But remember we are often distracted by things coming up, phone calls, e-mail's, texts, the internet. So the first strategy may prove more fruitful unless of course you are disciplined enough to set a time frame and stick to it.

The main aim is to analyse and understand your time and what you use it for and essentially the stronger the reason you have to do something the more likely you are to take the action. That might be obvious but sometimes we all need a little adjustment to our daily scales to tip them in to the balance which works best for us.

"Strong reasons make strong actions." - William Shakespeare

Too Old To Learn?

We are never to clever, too old, to rich, too knowledgeable or too any thing to learn.

Learn something new everyday if you can.

Maybe:-

A fact.

A line out of a book.

A poem.

A sum.

A recipe.

A country.

A new skill.

An updated one.

Absolutely anything counts.

> "We have to abandon the idea that schooling is something restricted to youth. How can it be, in a world where half the things a man knows at 20 are no longer true at 40 - and half the things he knows at 40 hadn't been discovered when he was 20? - Arthur C. Clarke.

The Eternal Quest.

Have you ever been searching? Or perhaps felt on an eternal searching quest?

Some people never have or maybe never will.

But for some it's a 'state' of being.

It could be an inner drive or intuitive journey.

At our core our spiritual quest for something true, real or deeply alive is a dual signal of our being truly alive and that our inner selves want more than what they are currently feeling.

Is it enough to just 'be'? To just accept today as it is and be happy and grateful?

Maybe it isn't that surprising, a more complex reasoning is required.

On one level, yes we should breath in the moment, feel the vibrancy of life, have gratitude and grace for this present moment. But of course, there could be more, we might have burning desires that haven't yet been tended too. We might seek or strive for something else or some other place.

A conscious balancing act is all we need be mindful to. That our duality is appropriate for our thriving times. In our hearts, we can feel love and happiness, in our minds, we can be ever curious, think and ask questions and in our spirits, we can search until we find home and until we know our place is just right.

Searching isn't such a bad thing. It is more of a crime to inhibit the soul, to procrastinate our spirits and to deny our innate curiosity.

There will be a reason for your journey, there always is.

> "Care more than others think wise,
>
> risk more than others think safe,
>
> dream more than others think practical,
>
> expect more than others think possible."
>
> - Howard Schultz

Care To The End.

"People usually fail when they are on the verge of success.

So give as much care to the end as to the beginning;

Then there will be no failure." - Lao Tzu

It all matters you know?

Every single step, every morsel, every little detail.

It is easy to become discouraged, understandable to be restless, forgivable to have your strength tested by others.

You can take a break, have a rest and a well deserved breather but so long as you keep chipping away over time you will have the end in sight.

If you give as much care and attention at the end as you did in the beginning, at the absolute very least you know you have done the job well, to the best of your ability and you can be proud of your achievement.

Whatever else happens to it once it is off in to the Universe we possibly might not yet know but you did your bit and you did a sterling job.

Well done.

Nothing.

Nothing is more important than you.

You are the entire Universe complete.

If, as you are, all of the Universe, then the Universe is the whole of us.

We must all be One, the collective ones to change, improve and develop.

To make a difference and create the magnificent utopia.

> **"You must be the change you wish to see in the world." - Mohandas (Mahatma) Gandhi**

Thank-you.

Thank-you for being you. Just to let you know you are super appreciated around here and it wouldn't be the same without you.

I'd also like to take the time now to thank-you for reading this book, without you there wouldn't be much point would there?

So I hope you continue to have a sensational and spectacular life ahead filled with many long years of wondrous experiences, tons of feedback and personal triumphs and victories.

Did you like reading a small note of appreciation? Hedging the bets a bit but you most likely did.

It's hard not to smile, when someone else smiles, it's hard not to say thanks when someone says thanks or appreciates you and it's very hard not to feel great when you receive a card, a gift or a bunch of flowers or a personal token from someone you know, your family, friends, your co-workers or your business colleagues.

Most people are busy and so they just don't think. It's not intentional or anything personal, they just have so much to do, it just doesn't occur to them.

But as you are super organised and think differently, you can lead by example can't you? In your personal diary, organiser or whatever you use to keep track. You can begin today, send a note or similar each week or each month to whomever you like, for whatever reason you like.

If you want to you can keep a record of whom you sent what to for future reference.

It has to be said and there's nothing wrong with feeling good about yourself and your actions, even a tiny bit smug but just you go ahead and give thanks and appreciation and see where it sends you. It can only lead to more good things ahead.

Index

A

Ability 42, 80, 121, 157, 190
Abundance 41, 78, 81, 139, 158, 159
Acceptance 182
Achievement 28
Action 2
Actions II, 21, 23, 46, 71, 87, 90, 117, 120, 126, 158, 186, 193
Adjustments 14
Ali, Muhammed 55, 81, 165
Alternative 28, 54, 137, 177
Ambitions 41, 60
Answer 31, 33, 51, 83, 115, 118, 142
Answers 28, 69, 150, 177
Anxieties 7
Approach 33, 54, 104, 168, 185
Aristotle 147
Aspirations 15, 75, 116
Aspire 62, 126
Attitude 21, 24, 115, 171

B

Balance 33, 34, 41, 74, 94, 95, 114, 125, 164, 176, 186
Balances 37
Balancing 32, 118, 188
Ban Breathnach, Sarah 105
Beautiful 6–207
Beckwith, Michael 11, 49, 198
Be, do or have 3, 28, 48, 66, 83, 156
Belief 31, 41, 42, 119, 165, 181, 184
Beliefs 10, 53, 60, 70, 116, 143
Believe 3, 5, 37, 48, 50, 52, 53, 81, 84, 94, 135, 147, 156, 157, 180
Believing 48
Better 6, 12, 15, 20, 32, 37, 46, 49, 51, 52, 53, 56, 72, 78, 79, 84, 87, 89, 95, 96, 110, 116, 121, 125, 136, 137, 144, 145, 155, 157, 160, 163, 165, 168, 169, 176, 179
Bliss 42, 184
Body 27, 64, 101, 115
Bothered 8, 14, 23, 24
Brain 23, 36, 82, 92, 168
Brande, Dorothea 179
Braver 18
Breathe 6, 10, 131

C

Calmness 16
Can-do 24
Carefree 114, 115
Carefully 2, 13, 71
Celebrate 13, 20, 57, 88, 161
Centered 15
Challenge 21, 51, 72, 78, 111, 135, 137
Challenging 17, 90
Change 8, 11, 12, 13, 21, 58, 69, 73, 78, 90, 108, 113, 120, 137, 143, 156, 158, 159, 165, 173, 191
Changes 39, 121, 173
Chinese Proverb 42
Choice 6, 7, 11, 36, 39, 46, 54, 58, 62, 70, 86, 100, 113, 121, 124, 162, 171, 175, 179
Choose 6, 11, 43, 54, 71, 73, 90, 91, 125, 158, 182
Chopra, Deepak 159
Circumstances 4, 79, 108, 109, 126, 144, 147, 149, 174
Clarke, Arthur C. 100, 188
Comfortable 101
Comfort zones 3
Community 73, 100, 137
Concentrate 24, 116
Confucius 7, 14
Confused 66, 120, 150
Conscious 11, 23, 24, 46, 136, 188
Consistent 27, 104, 116
Contentment 33
Control 24, 33, 46, 61, 86, 122, 126, 129, 147
Cooper, James F. 63
Courage 47, 69, 95
Create 2, 43, 129, 165, 191
Creative 61, 136
Crow, Native American Proverb 98
Culture 15, 15–207, 63, 70
Curiosity 9, 177, 189

D

Daydreaming 134
Daydreams 43
Decision 17, 36, 37, 39, 48, 78, 79, 98, 121, 124, 129, 137
Decisions 2, 21, 36, 37, 78, 79, 84, 120, 121, 170
Degree 26, 44, 125, 149
Delighted 30
Desire 46, 82, 83
Despair 26, 182
Destination 14, 76, 110
Determination 47
Diao, Tai Gong 161
Diary 38, 88, 123, 167, 168, 192

Difference 14, 29, 55, 61, 75, 85, 91, 100, 116, 117, 137, 143, 169, 170, 175, 179, 185, 191
Difficult 17, 117, 173, 183
Disappointment 26
Discipline 26, 47, 66, 86, 87, 125, 171
Distracted 66
Doubt 3, 97, 120
Doubts 89
Dream 1, 2, 43, 50, 81, 82
Dreams 2, 3, 15, 19, 55, 75, 80, 85, 91, 97, 102, 104, 116, 119, 139, 149, 163, 172
Dutch Proverb 59

E

Egyptian Wisdom 42
Einstein, Albert 58, 92
Elements 23
Emotions 21, 95, 129, 147, 149, 174, 183
Energy 11, 72, 80, 95, 114, 138, 151, 159, 176
Enlighten 40
Enlightenment 40, 64
Enthusiastic 8
Evolvement 13
Excellence 26
Excellent 26, 27, 141
Expect 17, 27, 37, 45, 52, 110, 149, 183, 185, 189
Expression 20

F

Fail 31, 104, 148, 179, 190
Failure 14, 153, 162, 163, 190
Failures 23
Faith 31, 55, 115
Fears 3, 89, 129, 149, 165
Feedback 23, 79, 153, 157, 162, 163
Feeling 5, 42, 66, 70, 78, 94, 101, 112, 120, 155, 166, 171, 188, 193
Felltham, Owen 91
Flow 9, 9–207, 31, 52, 54, 66, 72, 119, 120, 149, 159, 164, 170
Focus 12, 114, 117, 156, 161, 179
Foundations 15
Freedom 46, 47, 57, 125
Friend 3, 7, 12, 39, 65, 97, 110, 128, 129, 140
Fulfillment 33
Future 35, 53, 80, 108, 109, 111, 148, 156, 193

G

Gandhi, Mohandas (Mahatma) 57, 117, 157, 191
Genius 1, 62
Goals 14, 19, 22, 23, 25, 32, 35, 43, 69, 72, 75, 83, 91, 95, 102, 104, 116, 117,

    127, 133, 156, 172
Goethe, Johann Wolfgang von 1, 62
Grateful 74, 88, 131, 163, 171, 175, 188
Gratitude 64, 158, 171, 188
Great 46, 47, 48, 56, 57, 59, 65, 94, 98, 100, 127, 128, 169, 174, 176, 192
Greatness 9, 63, 75
Growing 10, 58, 70, 79, 100, 101, 103, 104, 119
Guide 31, 69

H

Habit 86, 121, 136, 168, 169, 174
Habits 10, 100
Habitually 27
Happier 35, 116, 155
Happiness 7, 33, 41, 64, 73, 94, 101, 144, 151, 189
Happy 9, 9–207, 13, 39, 64, 68, 74, 81, 99, 104, 115, 120, 138, 143, 144, 151, 174, 188
Harmony 33, 43, 94, 114, 117, 148, 170, 176
Hawking, Stephen 130
Head 10, 34, 35, 42, 70, 149, 163
Health 20, 94, 96, 115, 145, 158
Heart 2, 42, 78, 91, 99, 144
Hill, Napoleon 51, 163
Holistic 45
Holmes Jr, Oliver Wendell 101
Honest 143, 169
Hope 6, 58, 90, 114, 118
Hopi, Native American 145
Hopi, Native American Proverb 90

I

Ideas 46, 70, 99, 134, 156
Imagination 3, 80, 92, 93, 129
Impossible 62, 69, 90, 100, 179
Improvement 13, 39, 96, 143
Indomitable spirit 47
Inspiration I, 41, 42, 46, 66, 181
Inspired 23, 69, 75, 104, 156, 179
Inspiring 33, 182
Instruct 24
Integrity 153, 169
Intelligence 183
Intentions 83, 143
Intuition 36, 42, 69, 78, 94, 120, 132, 157, 169
Intuitive 36, 70, 79, 170, 188
Inuit 19
Invest 15, 185
Irving, Washington 111

J

Japanese Proverb 43
Jobs, Steve 29
Journal 12, 38, 42, 88, 100, 171
Journey 15, 66, 85, 95, 99, 111, 112, 131, 145, 183, 188, 189

K

Kanuri, Nigerian Proverb 140
Kinesthetic 63, 70
King Jr, Martin Luther 139
Knowing 42, 48, 49, 70, 130

L

Lack 48, 55, 66, 99, 104, 127, 138
Landon, Michael 2
Law of Attraction 52
Lead 31, 62, 69, 93, 137, 192, 193
Learning 58, 100, 101, 104, 130, 137
Lee, Bruce 48, 111, 194
Life 2, 3, 4, 7, 10, 14, 15, 17, 21, 37, 39, 42, 47, 49, 52, 55, 61, 64, 66, 68, 69, 71, 74, 76, 78, 90, 92, 94, 95, 97, 98, 102, 106, 111, 112, 116, 118, 119, 120, 126, 128, 131, 144, 147, 151, 156, 158, 161, 163, 169, 172, 174, 179, 183, 188, 192
Light 18, 62, 102, 128, 129
Limited 28, 98
List 12, 13, 23, 33, 38, 45, 81, 83, 84, 87, 102, 132, 133, 134, 155, 166, 167, 168, 174, 177, 184, 185
Listening 36, 59, 76
Live 2, 27, 37, 43, 55, 58, 71, 73, 81, 90, 97, 131, 143, 151, 181, 183
Looking 20, 26, 28, 60, 72, 82, 90, 123, 141, 162, 164

M

Manifested 104
Martial Arts 21, 180
Mediocrity 26, 63
Mind 7, 8, 12, 24, 27, 28, 36, 45, 46, 52, 60, 61, 72, 73, 84, 91, 92, 93, 101, 103, 110, 111, 112, 114, 115, 117, 119, 121, 125, 127, 134, 145, 146, 149, 162
Mindful I, II, 11, 39, 43, 47, 49, 52, 94, 96, 129, 149, 154, 170, 173, 188
Minds 45, 78, 120, 129, 136, 137, 174, 177, 189
Mindset 56, 80, 158
Mistake 56, 124
Morley, Christopher 142
Motivation IV, 41, 72, 106, 176
Motivational 44
Mountain 6
Move on 34, 76, 79, 80, 145, 179
Music 93

N

Native American Proverb 90, 98, 100
Negative 11, 104, 129, 157, 171, 185
Neng, Hui 41
Notes 33, 100, 113, 174

O

Oglala Sioux, Native American Proverb 148
Oneness 21
Opinions 9, 181
Opportunity 34, 80, 100, 138, 146, 157
Optimum 26, 97
Order 12, 42, 46, 92, 115, 135, 164, 167
Organised 86, 122, 123, 192
Organiser 38, 167, 168, 192
Outcomes 27, 47, 163
Overwhelmed 33, 66, 141, 170

P

Passionately 14, 147
Past 34, 108, 109, 111, 135, 148, 185
Path 42, 62, 64, 79, 91, 110, 127, 150
Patterns 38
Peace 16, 143
Peak 6
Perfect 7, 8, 20, 32, 37, 56, 84, 91, 95, 118, 128, 135, 165
Perseverance 42
Persistent 92, 104, 109, 173
Perspective 54, 79, 91, 137, 177
Philosopher 134
Philosophically 113
Plan 23, 24, 27, 47, 60, 75, 184
Planned 8
Positive 11, 24, 52, 99, 100, 104, 119, 121, 129, 137, 145, 151, 157, 158, 172, 176, 177
Possibilities 3, 3–207, 28, 61, 98, 130, 175
Power 1, 46, 49, 67, 91, 108, 113, 129
Precious 10, 86, 165, 182
Prepare 27
Present 35, 38, 64, 68, 71, 90, 91, 148, 188
Pressured 38
Priority 12, 84, 156, 167
Pritchard, Michael 130
Problem 20, 98, 99, 108, 135
Process 23, 33, 46, 51, 111
Proctor, Bob 52, 69, 75, 98, 171
Progress 17
Projects 32
Purity 9, 90

Purpose IV, 4, 41, 42, 47, 64, 69, 90, 91, 104, 110, 111, 146, 156, 169, 180, 181, 184
Purposefully 13, 91

Q

Quiet 4, 16, 45
Quit 44, 91, 104, 128, 163

R

Reality 10, 19, 146, 179, 182
Reason 4, 5, 37, 41, 77, 79, 99, 136, 146, 165, 179, 182, 183, 186, 189, 192
Recycle 100, 136
Regret 37
Relax 17, 135
Research 19, 22, 51, 75, 168
Resistance 185
Resolve 47
Responsibility II, 14, 23, 33, 124
Review 38, 70, 79, 100, 185
Risks 95
Robbins, Anthony 109
Route 26
Rules 13

S

Samurai Maxim 10
Sandburg, Carl 39
Satisfaction 33
Schuller, Robert H. 146
Schultz, Howard 189
Seeking 9, 106, 177
Self confidence 48, 78, 79
Self-discipline 47
Self education 183
Self esteem 48, 78, 84, 120, 138, 162
Self mastery 21
Shakespeare, William 186
Shenandoah, Native American Proverb 143
Shine 18, 139, 144, 181
Shining 18
Silence 16, 76, 93
Situation 21
Smile 10, 13, 17, 30, 74, 127, 155, 171, 192
Socrates 152
Solutions 28
Soul 16, 64, 71, 91, 145, 148, 189
Source 150, 159
Spirit 27, 47, 64, 101, 115, 177, 182
Spiritual II, 71, 96, 102, 145, 168, 171, 188

Star 18
Steiner, Rudolf 5, 139
Steps 14, 22, 41, 42, 49, 61, 82, 92, 117, 127, 128, 133, 179
Stillness 16
Strength 5, 28, 47, 190
Stress 166
Stressed 39
Stronger 18, 117, 125, 186
Student 130
Sub-conscious 23, 24
Success 14, 94, 97, 101, 127, 130, 163, 173, 190
Successful 52, 94, 120, 163, 173
Sunshine 35
Support 31, 45, 66, 140, 181
Supporting 17, 47, 158

T

Tao 21, 54, 72, 79, 91, 170
Task 13, 42, 47, 110, 168, 176
Teacher 130
Temperaments 183
Test 17, 21, 53
Thackeray, William Makepeace 35
Thinking 3, 20, 22, 28, 30, 37, 52, 54, 56, 66, 79, 97, 99, 117, 120, 125, 132, 177
Thoreau, Henry David 15
Thought 10, 20, 28, 44, 56, 69, 72, 97, 178
Time 5, 10, 13, 16, 20, 21, 23, 24, 27, 31, 32, 33, 34, 36, 37, 38, 39, 44, 45, 46,
      49, 51, 53, 54, 55, 56, 66, 69, 70, 72, 76, 77, 84, 85, 86, 87, 91, 92, 94,
      97, 100, 108, 112, 114, 116, 117, 120, 122, 124, 125, 127, 128, 130, 133,
      134, 137, 138, 140, 142, 143, 147, 148, 157, 160, 161, 165, 166, 167,
      168, 169, 170, 171, 177, 178, 179, 180, 181, 183, 184, 185, 186, 190, 192
Today 2, 8, 19, 22, 23, 29, 30, 35, 39, 51, 52, 58, 64, 75, 79, 85, 88, 105, 109,
      116, 117, 119, 125, 127, 128, 130, 132, 134, 139, 141, 148, 156, 158,
      166, 167, 169, 184, 185, 188, 192
Tracy, Brian 95
Transformational 28
Transitional 17
Tzu, Chuang 135
Tzu, Lao 31, 55, 72, 85, 139, 149, 164, 190
Tzu, Lieh 151
Tzu, Sun- 122

U

Ueshiba, Morihei 64
Uncomfortable 17, 101, 170, 179
Unhappy 39, 120
Unique 18
Universal 11
Universal Principles 52
Universe 6, 10, 15, 17, 18, 20, 24, 25, 47, 54, 56, 66, 77, 79, 93, 103, 108, 110,

113, 115, 119, 125, 127, 131, 134, 135, 149, 159, 164, 170, 171, 183, 190, 191

V

Value 38
Values 41, 60, 70, 95, 106, 116, 143, 147, 153, 156
Victories 13–207
Virgil 96
Vision 43, 69
Visual 46, 174

W

Wanting 24
Ward, William Arthur 3, 50, 157, 173
Warrior 180
Way 6, 7, 9, 10, 14, 15, 20, 21, 24, 25, 33, 35, 39, 41, 50, 52, 54, 56, 58, 60, 61, 62, 71, 73, 75, 81, 88, 89, 90, 92, 99, 100, 102, 110, 112, 113, 115, 116, 127, 128, 133, 134, 135, 136, 139, 142, 144, 145, 146, 147, 149, 150, 151, 163, 165, 167, 168, 170, 171, 177, 178, 182, 183
Wilkins, Richard 83
Will 46, 90, 178
Wisdom I, II, 16, 40, 42, 47, 74, 90, 91, 138, 154, 174
Wish 34, 35, 46, 47, 71, 81, 125, 134, 191, 192
Wolof, Senegal Proverb 89
Wonder 6, 8, 17, 37, 90, 116, 148, 152, 160
Woolgathering 134
Working 26, 44, 76, 92, 134, 167
Worry 7, 8, 15, 24, 91, 114, 115, 156, 178, 182
Wu wei 170

Y

Year planner 60, 61
Yin yang 11, 76, 164, 169
Yogananda, Paramahansa 144

Z

Zen 9, 16, 54, 177
Zen Koan 9
Zen Proverb 16, 177
Ziglar, Zig 94

You Are Cordially Invited.

To continue on your amazing journey and find out more by visiting online where you will find:-

- A thought-provoking "Quote of the Day".

- How to subscribe to updates via email or RSS

- Weekly posts on all things mindful wisdom.

- Information about future events, seminars and more.

- How to join the online membership community.

- Keep up-to-date and join in on Facebook and Twitter

- Shop for inspirational items and gifts.

www.mindful-wisdom.com

Lightning Source UK Ltd.
Milton Keynes UK
UKOW06f2056171115

262929UK00003B/5/P